G. SCHIRMER
COLLECTION
OPERA LIBRETTOS

TOSCA

Music by
Giacomo Puccini

Libretto by
GIUSEPPE GIACOSA and LUIGI ILLICA
After the play by VICTORIEN SARDOU

English Version
by
JOHN GUTMAN

Ed. 2238

G. SCHIRMER, Inc.

Important Notice

Performances of this opera must be licensed by the publisher.

All rights of any kind with respect to this opera and any parts thereof, including but not limited to stage, radio, television, motion picture, mechanical reproduction, translation, printing, and selling are strictly reserved.

License to perform this work, in whole or in part, whether with instrumental or keyboard accompaniment, must be secured in writing from the Publisher. Terms will be quoted upon request.

Copying of either separate parts or the whole of this work, by hand or by any other process, is unlawful and punishable under the provisions of the U.S.A. Copyright Act.

The use of any copies, including arrangements and orchestrations, other than those issued by the Publisher, is forbidden.

All inquiries should be directed to the Publisher:

G. Schirmer Rental Department
5 Bellvale Road
Chester, NY 10918
(914) 469-2271

Copyright © 1956 by G. Schirmer, Inc. (ASCAP) New York, NY
International Copyright Secured. All Rights Reserved.
**Warning: Unauthorized reproduction of this publication is
prohibited by Federal law and subject to criminal prosecution.**

TOSCA

Tosca is the product of Puccini's most fruitful period. At thirty-eight, the composer had known success with *Manon Lescaut* and *Bohème* when, in the spring of 1896, he started to work on the new opera. Though certain ideas recur throughout his works, he sensed the need to vary the types of story and locale in which these ideas were presented; thus, after the hotly romantic *Manon* and gently lyrical *Bohème,* he felt himself due to create a full-blooded veristic melodrama.

Despite previous experience in contending with rival composers for a subject he wanted, Puccini had yet to face a temperamental playwright. When he journeyed to Paris to stage *La Bohème*, he confronted Victorien Sardou, sixty-five-year-old dean of the French theater, author of *La Tosca*. Even the most famous of non-operatic Toscas, Sarah Bernhardt, always addressed Sardou as "dear master."

Puccini held his ground in pressing for modifications, which included the elimination of an entire act; in the end, Sardou hailed the opera and did his best to boss its Paris premiere in 1903.

Puccini's librettists, Giacosa and Illica, the same pair he had worked with on *La Bohème,* found this collaboration generally smoother. The libretto, so strong dramatically that early critics found it swamped the music, had been hailed by even the aged Giuseppe Verdi.

A restless atmosphere preceded the world premiere of *Tosca* in Rome on January 14, 1900. Many felt that Puccini, having enjoyed such success, ought to be cut down to size. Further, the Roman public was prepared to eye askance a work by an out-of-town composer who had the temerity to set his opera's action on their very doorstep. Then as now, Sant' Andrea Church, The Farnese Palace and Sant' Angelo Castle figured as integral parts of the Roman landscape. The characters of *Tosca,* as well as the events that shape its action, had roots in historical fact.

Despite a false bomb scare and a near-riot instigated by disgruntled latecomers trying to gain their seats, *Tosca* was performed — by Romanian diva Ericlea Darclée, tenor Emilio de Marchi and baritone Eugenio Giraldoni, with Leopoldo Mugnone on the podium. The reception was mixed, but the new opera went on to establish itself in short order. Its American premiere, at the Metropolitan (February 4, 1901), starred Milka Ternina, Giuseppe Cremonini and Antonio Scotti, Luigi Mancinelli conducting.

Courtesy of Opera News

THE STORY

ACT I. Cesare Angelotti, former consul of the Roman republic freshly escaped from the Castle of St. Angelo, where he has been held as a political prisoner, seeks refuge in the Attavanti Chapel of the majestic church of *Sant' Andrea della Valle*. Hardly has he concealed himself when the ancient Sacristan of the church shuffles in followed by the painter Mario Cavaradossi, who admits that his portrait of the Madonna on the wall was inspired not only by a model but by his beloved Floria Tosca, a famous singer of Rome. When the Sacristan leaves, Angelotti ventures out, but his friend Cavaradossi, thrusting a lunch basket in his hands, hurries him away as Tosca makes her entrance. She pleads with the painter for a rendezvous in the country and then, noticing the beautiful and lifelike Madonna, jealously suspects the worst. Cavaradossi reassures her that with eyes like her own, Tosca has nothing to fear from another woman. When she departs, Cavaradossi summons his friend and takes him off to hide at his villa. Meanwhile the Sacristan returns with a crowd of choir-boys, whose frolickings are interrupted by the majestic entrance of Baron Scarpia, head of the Roman police, in search of Angelotti. When Tosca returns to meet her lover she finds instead the cynical but amorous Scarpia who, unmoved by the religious procession and *Te Deum* which follow, plays on her jealousy, planting in her mind false doubts concerning the love of Cavaradossi, whom the Baron secretly vows he will send to the scaffold so that he may possess Tosca himself.

ACT II. In his magnificent apartment in the Farnese Palace, Scarpia anticipates the pleasure of bending the fiery Tosca to his will. His agents Sciarrone and Spoletta bring in Cavaradossi, now in custody for protecting Angelotti, as Tosca's voice is heard from the concert in Queen Caroline's apartment below. When the painter refuses to give any information on his friend he is led away to the adjacent torture-chamber, just as Tosca arrives dressed in her gala robes. While the groans of Cavaradossi issue from the next room, Scarpia questions Tosca and finally succeeds in prying from her the name of Angelotti's hiding place. Cavaradossi is at once released and led in, bleeding. Discovering that Tosca has revealed the hiding place, he curses her and cries defiance at the tyranny of Scarpia and the foreign oppressors he represents. Furiously Scarpia orders his minions to remove the painter. Alone with Tosca, the Baron bargains with her for Cavaradossi's life. Vainly she pleads for mercy, protesting that she has never done anything to deserve being faced with such a terrible proposition. Finally Tosca promises to yield to Scarpia's advances as the price of her lover's freedom. Scarpia summons Spoletta and orders a mock execution for Cavaradossi, after which he will be free. No sooner has he written out a passport for herself and her lover than Tosca stabs him, and placing a crucifix on his breast and candles at his head and feet, slips away.

ACT III. On the battlements of the Castle of Sant' Angelo, the voice of a distant shepherd is heard at dawn while one by one the bells of Rome strike the hour. Soon Cavaradossi is led in to a waiting jailer, whom he bribes to obtain permission for a last letter to Tosca. She hurries in and tells him of Scarpia's murder and of the simulated execution. He can hardly believe the news and looks in wonder at the soft hands that dared so much to save him. The lovers ecstatically plan for the future. As the firing squad advances and draws, Tosca retires with a final word to Cavaradossi about how to fall realistically. The soldiers fire and file out. When they have gone she hurries to the painter's side and is horrified to find that the execution was real after all: Scarpia betrayed his promise. Distant shouts announce that the Baron's murder is discovered. As Spoletta and Sciarrone rush in, the despairing Tosca leaps over the battlement to her death.

Courtesy of Opera News

CAST OF CHARACTERS

FLORIA TOSCA, an opera singer . . . . Soprano

MARIO CAVARADOSSI, a painter . . . . Tenor

BARON SCARPIA, the chief of the Roman police . . . . Baritone

CESARE ANGELOTTI, an underground fighter . . . . Bass

A SACRISTAN . . . . Baritone

SPOLETTA, a police agent . . . . Tenor

SCIARRONE, Baron Scarpia's orderly . . . . Bass

A JAILER . . . . Bass

A SHEPHERD BOY . . . . Soprano

A Cardinal; A Judge; Roberti, Executioner; A Scribe; An Officer; A Sergeant; Soldiers; Police-Agents; Ladies; Nobles; Citizens.

Rome: June 1800

SYNOPSIS OF SCENES

		Page
Act I	The Church of Sant' Andrea della Valle	1
Act II	Palazzo Farnese	18
Act III	Castel Sant' Angelo	35

TOSCA

ATTO PRIMO

La Chiesa di Sant'Andrea della Valle.

(A destra la Cappella Attavanti. A sinistra un impalcato: su di esso un gran quadro coperto da tela. Attrezzi vari da pittore. Un paniere.)

ANGELOTTI

(vesito da prigioniero, lacero, sfatto, tremante dalla paura, entra ansante, quasi correndo, dalla porta laterale. Dà una rapida occhiata intorno)
Ah!... Finalmente!... Nel terror mio stolto
vedea ceffi di birro in ogni volto.
(torna a guardare attentamente intorno a sè con più calma a riconoscere il luogo. — Dà un sospiro di sollievo vedendo la colonna colla pila dell'acqua santa e la Madonna)
La pila... la colonna...
"A piè della Madonna"
mi scrisse mia sorella...
(si si avvicina, cerca ai piedi della Madonna e ne ritira, con un soffocato grido di gioia, una chiave)
Ecco la chiave... ed ecco la cappella!...
(addita la Cappella Attavanti; con gran precauzione introduce la chiave nella serratura, apre la cancellata, penetra nella Cappella, rinchiude... e scompare).

IL SAGRESTANO

(entra dal fondo tenendo fra le mani un mazzo di pennelli e parlando ad alta voce come se rivolgesse la parola a qualcuno)
E frega e lava!... Ogni pennello è sozzo
peggio che il collarin d'uno scagnozzo.
Signor pittore... Tò!...
(guarda verso l'impalcato dove sta il quadro, e vedendolo deserto, esclama sorpreso)
Nessuno. — Avrei giurato
che fosse ritornato
il cavalier Cavaradossi.
(depone i pennelli, sale sull'impalcato, guarda dentro il paniere e dice)
No,
sbaglio. — Il paniere è intatto.
(suona l'Angelus. Il Sagrestano si inginocchia e prega sommesso)

CAVARADOSSI

(dalla porta laterale, vedendo il Sagrestano in ginocchio)
Che fai?

SAGRESTANO

(alzandosi)
Recito l'*Angelus*.

TOSCA

ACT I

Scene: The Church of Sant'Andrea della Valle

(At the right, the Attavanti Chapel. A dais on the left: on it, a large picture on an easel covered by a piece of cloth. Painter's tools lie about; also a basket. Angelotti enters looking like a prisoner, emaciated, exhausted, trembling with fear, breathing heavily. He surveys the scene with a rapid glance.)

ANGELOTTI

Ah! I can breathe now . . . Terrifying faces
everywhere . . . in the most unlikely places!
(He gives a start, then takes a careful look as though reconnoitering the scene. Seeing the pillar with the holy water basin and the Madonna, he heaves a sigh of relief.)
The basin and the pillar . . .
and this is the Madonna
my sister said to look for.
(Going closer to the pillar, Angelotti looks for the key at the foot of the Madonna. Not finding it, he goes on searching in great excitement. With a gesture of discouragement he starts looking for the key again. Finally he finds the key, suppressing a joyful outcry.)
Here is the key,
(pointing to the Attavanti Chapel)
And this must be the chapel.
(Frightened again to be discovered, he glances around, then walks over to the chapel, very cautiously inserts the key, opens the gate and disappears after having locked the gate again.
The Sacristan appears at the back; moving from right to left, he begins to attend to his chores. He carries a bunch of paint brushes. He walks up to the dais, speaking aloud as though talking to somebody.)

SACRISTAN

(He has a nervous tic; a quick twitch of the neck and the shoulders.)
I clean his brushes; that is my favorite pastime!
Yet they are always filthier than the last time.
Signor, good morning!
(Looking at the dais, he is surprised at finding it empty.)
What? No painter?
And I was certain that I had heard his footsteps,
my noble friend, Cavaradossi.
(He puts down his paint brushes and climbs on the dais, peering into the basket.)
No, curious.
No one touched the basket.
(He comes down from the dais. The Angelus is being rung. The Sacristan kneels down and prays humbly.
Cavaradossi comes in through the side door; he sees the Sacristan kneeling.)

CAVARADOSSI

What's this?

SACRISTAN *(getting up)*

Saying an Angelus.

(Cavaradossi sale sull'impalcato e scopre il quadro. E una Maria Maddalena a grandi occhi azzuri. con una gran pioggia di capelli dorati. Il pittore vi sta dinanzi muto attentamente osservando.
Il Sagrestano, volgendosi verso Cavaradossi per dirigergli la parola, vede il quadro scoperto e dà in un grido di meraviglia.)
O sante
ampolle! Il suo ritratto!...

CAVARADOSSI

Di chi?

SAGRESTANO

Di quell'ignota
che i dì passati a pregar qui venìa
tutta devota — e pia.
(e accenna verso la Madonna dalla quale Angelotti trasse la chiave)

CAVARADOSSI

(sorridendo)
E vero. E tanto ell'era
infervorata nella sua preghiera
ch'io ne pinsi, non visto, il bel sembiante.

SAGRESTANO

(Fuori, Satana, fuori!)

CAVARADOSSI

Dammi i colori!
(Il Sagrestano eseguisce. Cavaradossi dipinge con rapidità e si sofferma spesso a riguardare: il Sagrestano va e viene, portando una catinella entro la quale continua a lavare i pennelli.
A un tratto Cavaradossi si ristà di dipingere; leva di tasca un medaglione contenente una miniatura e gli occhi suoi vanno dal medaglione al quadro.)

CAVARADOSSI	SAGRESTANO
Recondita armonia	*(fra sè, brontolando)*
di belleze diverse!... È bruna Floria,	(Scherza coi fanti e lascia stare i santi.
l'ardente amante mia,	Queste diverse gonne
e te, beltade ignota	che fanno concorrenza alle Madonne
cinta di chiome bionde!	mandan tanfo d'inferno.
Tu azzurro hai l'occhio, Tosca ha l'occhio nero!	
L'arte nel suo mistero	
le diverse bellezze insiem confonde:	
ma nel ritrar costei	
il mio solo pensier, Tosca tu sei!	

(Cavaradossi steps on the dais and uncovers the picture: a painting of Mary Magdalen with big blue eyes and golden hair to her shoulders. He gazes at the picture with silent attention. The Sacristan is about to speak to Cavaradossi, he sees the painting and exclaims in great astonishment)
Goodness gracious! I know that lady.

CAVARADOSSI *(to the Sacristan)*

You do?

SACRISTAN

That lovely stranger; the past few mornings
she's come here to worship
(pointing to the statue of the Madonna where Angelotti had found the key)
with great devotion and feeling.

CAVARADOSSI *(smiling)*

I've seen her.
She was so lost to all around her that she never saw me
all the time I was painting her lovely features.

SACRISTAN *(shocked)*

Satan, get thee behind me!

CAVARADOSSI *(to the Sacristan, who does as he is told)*

Give me my brushes.
(Cavaradossi starts to paint, interrupts himself often to scrutinize his work, while the Sacristan, sitting at the foot of the dais, begins his chores. Cavaradossi again interrupts his painting: takes out of his pocket a medallion, and his eyes begin to wander from the miniature in the medallion to the painting.)
In strange mysterious fashion
beauty's face is eternal.
My Tosca burns with love,
aglow with flaming passion.

SACRISTAN *(mumbling to himself)*

Once she's been painted, they will get acquainted.
(He goes to find some water for his work.)

CAVARADOSSI

My lovely stranger is mild as spring,
golden curls on her shoulder,
eyes as blue as heaven;
dark as night are Tosca's.

SACRISTAN *(returns and says, with indignation)*

Once she's been painted, they will get acquainted.
(He starts cleaning his brushes again.)

CAVARADOSSI

Art, with a spell of magic,
makes the two seem like one
to the beholder.
My art knows many faces,
but my heart never changes:
I have vowed my love to you,
Tosca, to you!
(continues his painting)

SACRISTAN

It's this one, or another.
They all presume
to rival the Holy Mother.
What a stench of damnation!

SAGRESTANO

Ma con quei cani — di volterriani
nemici del santissimo governo
non c'è da metter voce!...
Facciam piuttosto il segno della croce).
(a Cavaradossi)
Vado, Eccellenza?

CAVARADOSSI

Fa il tuo piacere! *(ritorna a dipingere).*

SAGRESTANO

(indicando il cesto)
Pieno è il paniere...
Fa penitenza?

CAVARADOSSI

Fame non ho.

SAGRESTANO

(con ironia stropicciandosi le mani)
Oh!... mi rincresce!
(non può trattenere un gesto di gioia e uno sguardo di avidità verso il cesto che prende ponendolo un po' in disparte)
Badi, quand'esce
chiuda.

CAVARADOSSI

Va!

SAGRESTANO

Vo.
(s'allontana per il fondo)
(Cavaradossi volgendo le spalle alla Cappella lavora. Angelotti, credendo deserta la chiesa, appare dietro la cancellata e introduce a chiave per aprire.)

CAVARADOSSI

(al cigolio della serratura si volta)
Gente là dentro!
((al movimento fatto da Cavaradossi, Angelotti, atterito si arresta come per rifugiarsi ancora nella Cappella — ma — alzati gli occhi, un grido di gioia, che egli soffoca tosto timoroso, erompe dal suo petto. Egli ha riconosciuto il pittore e gli stende le braccia come ad un aiuto insperato)

ANGELOTTI

Voi! Cavaradossi!
Vi manda Iddio!

CAVARADOSSI

Ma...

ANGELOTTI

(va fin sotto l'impalcato)
Non mi ravvisate?
Il carcere mi ha dunque assai mutato

CAVARADOSSI

SACRISTAN *(dries the brushes and goes on mumbling)*
Once she's been painted, they will get acquainted.
He worships reason and that is treason!
He laughs at all we hold in veneration.
Such people are a danger!
Once she's been painted, they will get acquainted!
Such doings in a place that should be sainted!
(He deposits his bucket under the dais and puts the brushes in a jug close to the painter.)
(pointing at Cavaradossi) I think I'd better treat him like a stranger.
(to Cavaradossi) Excellency, may I?

CAVARADOSSI
I do not need you. *(continues painting)*

SACRISTAN
Here is your basket. Aren't you eating?

CAVARADOSSI
No, I won't eat.

SACRISTAN
No? I am sorry.
(He rubs his hands ironically; cannot suppress a joyful gesture and a greedy look at the basket, which he puts aside carefully. He then takes a pinch of snuff.)
Do not forget to lock up!

CAVARADOSSI *(busy painting)*
Go!

SACRISTAN *(leaving)*
Good.
(Cavaradossi paints, turning his back to the chapel. Angelotti, assuming the church to be empty, appears behind the gate and is about to open it. Cavaradossi, hearing the key in the lock, turns around.)

CAVARADOSSI
What can that noise be?
(Angelotti, terrified by Cavaradossi's movement, stops and wonders if he had better hide in the chapel again, but looking up he finds it hard not to cry out with joy: he has recognized Cavaradossi and stretches his arms towards him, delighted to find unexpected help.)

ANGELOTTI
You! Cavaradossi!
(Cavaradossi does not recognize him and remains on his dais in amazement.)
God must have sent you!
(Angelotti steps up to him so that he may recognize him.)
You don't seem to know me?
Has prison really changed me so completely?

(Cavaradossi guarda fiso il volto di Angelotti, e finalmente lo ravvisa. Depone rapido tavolozza e pennelli, scende dall'impalcato verso Angelotti, guardandosi cauto intorno)
Angelotti!

ANGELOTTI

Appunto.

CAVARADOSSI

Il Console
della spenta repubblica romana.
(corre a chiudere la porta a destra)

ANGELOTTI

Fuggii pur ora da Castel Sant'Angelo ...

CAVARADOSSI

Disponete di me.

VOCE DI TOSCA

Mario!
(alla voce di Tosca, Cavaradossi fa un rapido cenno ad Angelotti di tacere)

CAVARADOSSI

Celatevi!
È una donna ... gelosa. Un breve istante
e la rimando.

VOCE DI TOSCA

Mario!

CAVARADOSSI

(verso la porta da dove viene la voce di Tosca)
Eccomi!

ANGELOTTI

(colto da un accesso di debolezza si appoggia all'implicato)
Sono
Stremo di forze — non mi reggo.

CAVARADOSSI

(rapidissimo, sale sull'impalcato, ne discende col paniere e incoraggiando Angelotti, lo spinge verso la Cappella)
In questo
panier vi è cibo e vino.

ANGELOTTI

Grazie!

CAVARADOSSI

Presto!
(Angelotti entra nella Cappella.)

VOCE DI TOSCA

(chiamando ripetutamente stizzita)
Mario!

CAVARADOSSI

(apre)
Son qui!
(Tosca entra con una specie di violenza, allontana bruscamente Mario che vuole abbracciarla e guarda sospettosa intorno a sè)

(Cavaradossi, recognizing him, quickly puts down his palette and brush and comes down from the dais towards Angelotti.)

CAVARADOSSI

Angelotti!
The governor of the overthrown Roman republic!
(He hastily locks the side entrance.)

ANGELOTTI
(walking up to Cavaradossi; in a whisper)
I have escaped at last from Fort Sant'Angelo.

CAVARADOSSI *(magnanimously)*
Tell me what I can do!

TOSCA *(outside the church door)*
Mario!
(Hearing Tosca's voice, Cavaradossi motions to Angelotti to be silent.)

CAVARADOSSI

Go hide yourself.
I don't want her to see you.
I will be with you in a moment.

TOSCA

Mario!

CAVARADOSSI
(speaking towards the door from where Tosca's voice is heard)
Here I am.
(Angelotti, growing faint, leans against the dais and moans.)

ANGELOTTI

I can't stand it much longer, I'm exhausted . . .
(Cavaradossi quickly grasps the basket and hands it to Angelotti.)

CAVARADOSSI

There's food and some wine here in this basket.

ANGELOTTI

Thank you.

CAVARADOSSI
(He urges Angelotti to hide in the chapel.)
Hurry!
(Angelotti disappears into the chapel.)

TOSCA *(annoyed)*
Mario! Mario! Mario!

CAVARADOSSI *(opens the door with feigned calm)*
I'm here.
(Tosca storms in and looks around suspiciously. Cavaradossi wants to embrace her but she wards him off.)

TOSCA
Perchè chiuso?

CAVARADOSSI
Lo vuole
il Sagrestano.

TOSCA
A chi parlavi?

CAVARADOSSI
A te!

TOSCA
Altre parole bisbigliavi. Ov'è?...

CAVARADOSSI
Chi?

TOSCA
Colei!... Quella donna!...
Ho udito i lesti
passi e un fruscìo di vesti...

CAVARADOSSI
Sogni!

TOSCA
Lo neghi?

CAVARADOSSI
Lo nego e t'amo! *(per baciarla)*

TOSCA
(con dolce rimprovero)
Oh! innanzi alla madonna.
Lascia pria ch'io l'infiori e che la preghi.
(si avvicina alla Madonna, dispone con arte, intorno ad essa i fiori che ha portato con sè, si inginocchia e prega con molta devozione, poi s'alza)
(a Cavaradossi, che si è avviato per riprendere il lavoro)
Ora stammi a sentire — stassera canto,
ma è spettacolo breve. — Tu mi aspetti
sull'uscio della scena
e alla tua villa andiam, soli, soletti.

CAVARADOSSI
(che fu sempre soprapensieri)
Stassera?!

TOSCA
E luna piena   piena
ed il notturno effluvio floreale
inebria il cor. — Non sei contento?

CAVARADOSSI
(ancora un po' distratto e peritoso)
Tanto!

TOSCA
(colpita da quell'accento)
Tornalo a dir!

TOSCA
Why's the door locked?

CAVARADOSSI *(pretending indifference)*
The Sacristan insisted.

TOSCA
I heard you speaking . . .

CAVARADOSSI
To you!

TOSCA
No, no, I'm sure I heard some whispering.
She's here.

CAVARADOSSI
Who?

TOSCA
You know . . . that woman!
I heard a woman's step
and the rustling of a silk dress!

CAVARADOSSI
Nonsense!

TOSCA
Deny it!

CAVARADOSSI *(with passion)*
I do! I love you.
(tries to kiss Tosca.)

TOSCA *(with a mild reproach)*
Oh, the Holy Mother sees us.
No, Mario, no!
Let me offer my prayers and my flowers.
(She walks slowly up to the Madonna and places her flowers at the Madonna's feet; then kneels and offers a fervent prayer. She blesses herself and gets up. To Cavaradossi, who has returned to his work.)
Can you meet me tonight?
I've a performance but I'm through very early.
I'll expect you as soon as it is over,
and we will go away . . .
you and I, together.

CAVARADOSSI *(absent-mindedly)*
This evening?

TOSCA
There will be moonlight,
and the fragrant perfume of the night,
for us alone.
Won't that be lovely?
(She sits down at the foot of the dais close to Cavaradossi.)

CAVARADOSSI *(hardly paying attention)*
Lovely!

TOSCA *(shocked by his coolness)*
Say it again.

CAVARADOSSI

Tanto!

TOSCA

Lo dici male:
(va a sedere sulla gradinata presso a Cavaradossi)
non la sospiri la nostra casetta
che tutta ascosa nel verde ci aspetta?
nido a noi sacro, ignoto al mondo inter.
pien d'amore e di mister?
    Oh al tuo fianco sentire
        per le silenziose
        stellate ombre, salire
        le voci delle cose!
    Dai boschi, dai roveti,
        dall'arse erbe, dall'imo
        dei franti sepolcreti
        odorosi di timo,
    la notte escon bisbigli
        di minuscoli amori
        e perfidi consigli
        che ammolliscono i cuori.
Fiorite, o campi immensi, palpitate
aure marine nel lunare albor,
piovete voluttà, vôlte stellate!
Arde a Tosca nel sangue il folle amor!

CAVARADOSSI

(vinto, ma vigilante)
Mi avvinci ne'tuoi lacci!...
Mia sirena! Verrò.
(guarda verso la parte donde uscì Angelotti)
Ma or lasciami al lavoro.

TOSCA

Mi discacci?

CAVARADOSSI

Urge l'opra, lo sai!

TOSCA

Vado! *(alza gli occhi e vede il quadro)*
Chi è quella
donna bionda lassù?

CAVARADOSSI

La Maddalena.
Ti piace?

CAVARADOSSI

Lovely!

TOSCA *(irritated)*

You do not mean it! You do not mean it!
Deep in the woods there's a house that will hide us,
give us the rest that the world has denied us.
No one will find us in our secret nest,
Love alone will be our guest.
You and I, night and silence, crickets in the garden,
and high up in a tree
a nightingale singing for you and me.
The sweetest fragrance billows
from trees and flowers. An arbor
amidst the weeping willows
will be our harbor
for lovers' secret sessions;
and the moon, that discovers
those amorous confessions,
winks and smiles at the lovers.
The stars will light our faces,
and the night will be throbbing with music . . .
a wondrous singing in the midnight sky.
Ah, you'll hold me in your passionate embraces,
and the world will pass us by.

CAVARADOSSI

Ah! You've enslaved my heart forever.
Lovely Tosca!

TOSCA *(with complete abandon)*

I'm your Tosca, I'm yours forevermore.

CAVARADOSSI

How I long for tonight!

TOSCA

I adore you.
(Resting her head on Cavaradossi's shoulder, who suddenly draws back, looking towards the gate through which Angelotti disappeared.)

CAVARADOSSI

Now leave me to my painting.

TOSCA *(surprised)*

Must I leave you?

CAVARADOSSI

It's the picture, you see.

TOSCA *(gets up, annoyed)*

Well then, ciao!
(Moving away from Cavaradossi, then turning around she sees the painting and rushes back toward him in great agitation.)
And who is the lovely woman up there?

CAVARADOSSI *(calmly)*

The Holy Virgin. You like it?

TOSCA
È troppo bella!

CAVARADOSSI
(ridendo ed inchinandosi)
Prezioso elogio.

TOSCA
(sospettosa)
Ridi?
Quegli occhi cilestrini io già li vidi...

CAVARADOSSI
(con indifferenza)
Ce n'è tanti pel mondo!

TOSCA
(cercando di ricordare)
Aspetta... Aspetta...
È l'Attavanti!

CAVARADOSSI
(ridendo)
Brava!

TOSCA
(cieca di gelosia)
La vedi? Ti ama? Tu l'ami? Quei passi,
quel bisbiglio... Qui stava
pur ora! Ah la civetta!
A me!

CAVARADOSSI
(serio)
La vidi ieri — ma fu puro
caso. A pregar qui venne...
non visto la ritrassi.

TOSCA
Giura!

CAVARADOSSI
(serio)
Giuro!

TOSCA
(sempre cogli occhi rivolti al quadro)
Come mi guarda
fiso!

CAVARADOSSI
(la spinge dolcemente a scendere dalla gradinata. Essa discende all'indietro tenendo alto le sue mani in quelle di Cavaradossi. Tosca scendendo ha sempre la faccia verso il quadro cui Mario dà le spalle)
Vien via...

TOSCA
Di me, beffarda,
ride. *(sono scesi)*

CAVARADOSSI
Follia! *(la tiene presso di sè fissandola in viso)*

TOSCA
She's much too lovely.
CAVARADOSSI *(laughs and bows)*
You're very flattering.
TOSCA *(suspiciously)*
Flattering? Those skyblue eyes . . .
I know I've seen them somewhere.

CAVARADOSSI *(nonchalantly)*
They are nothing unusual.

TOSCA *(searching her memory)*
Where was it? I know her.
(walks up towards the picture, triumphantly exclaiming:)
It's L'Attavanti!
CAVARADOSSI *(laughs)*
Bravo.
TOSCA *(overcome by jealousy)*
She knows you, loves you?
(she cries) You love her? You love her?

CAVARADOSSI *(trying to calm her)*
I never met her.
TOSCA *(does not listen; furiously jealous)*
Those footsteps . . . that secret whispering . . .
Ah, you saw her this morning!
CAVARADOSSI
You're raving!
TOSCA
It's true, it's true.
You have betrayed me!
CAVARADOSSI *(seriously)*
It's true, I saw her, yet I never met her.
She came here to worship;
she never even saw me.
TOSCA
Swear it!
CAVARADOSSI *(solemnly)*
Gladly!
TOSCA *(with her eyes still on the painting)*
Look how these eyes defy me!

CAVARADOSSI *(gently urging her to leave the dais)*
Please go now!
TOSCA
She stares at me and mocks me.
(She walks backwards away from the picture with her hands in Cavaradossi's hands, but never taking her eyes off the picture. Cavaradossi holds Tosca close and looks into her eyes.)
CAVARADOSSI
What nonsense!

TOSCA
(insistente)
Ah, quegli occhi . . . quegli occhi! . . .

CAVARADOSSI
Quale occhio al mondo può star di paro
all'ardente occhio tuo nero?
E qui che l'esser mio s'affisa intero.
Occhio all'amor soave, all'ira fiero
qual altro al mondo può star di paro
all'occhio tuo nero?

TOSCA
(rapita, appoggiando la testa alla spalla di Cavaradossi)
Oh come la sai bene
l'arte di farti amare! . . .
(sempre insistendo nella sua idea)
Ma . . . falle gli occhi neri!

CAVARADOSSI
Mia gelosa!

TOSCA
Sì, lo sento . . . ti tormento
senza posa.

CAVARADOSSI
Mia gelosa!

TOSCA
Certa sono — del perdono
se tu guardi al mio dolor!

CAVARADOSSI
Tosca idolatrata
Ogni cosa in te mi piace;
l'ira audace
e lo spasimo d'amor!

TOSCA
Dilla ancora
la parola che consola . . .
dilla ancora!

CAVARADOSSI
Mia vita, amante inquieta,
dirò sempre: "Floria, t'amo!"
L'alma acquieta
sempre "T'amo!" ti dirò!

TOSCA
(sciogliendosi, paurosa d'esser vinta)
Vado, Eccellenza?
Dio, Dio! quante peccata!
M'hai tutta spettinata.

CAVARADOSSI
Or va — lasciami!

TOSCA
Tu fino a stassera
sta lì, fermo al lavoro. E mi prometti

TOSCA *(gently upbraids him)*

Ah, those eyes!

CAVARADOSSI

I've never seen other eyes so lovely
as your ardent dark eyes, my Tosca.
Eyes that have seared my heart
and have engraved there your beauty forever.
Eyes now aglow with passion, now afire with fury.
No other eyes in this world can rival your beautiful dark eyes.

TOSCA *(enraptured, she rests her head on his shoulder)*

One word from you, my darling,
and I can doubt no longer!
But . . . *(with malice)* won't you paint her eyes dark?

CAVARADOSSI *(tenderly)*

You are jealous!

TOSCA

Yes, I'm guilty. I confess that I am jealous!

CAVARADOSSI

Lovely Tosca . . .

TOSCA

But I'm certain you'll forgive me
when you know the grief in my heart.

CAVARADOSSI

My Tosca, whom I worship,
who alone makes life worth living,
I'll forgive you, for I know the grief in your heart.

TOSCA

Tell me love's unending story in its glory!
Say you love me.

CAVARADOSSI

My darling, my beloved,
do believe me. I adore you.
This love I gave you
shall not die until I die.

TOSCA *(drawing away)*

Oh, is nothing sacred?
You see what you have done now?

CAVARADOSSI

But, please, leave me now!

TOSCA

You say you will work here all day at your painting?

che sia caso o fortuna,
sia treccia bionda o nera,
a pregar non verrà, donna nessuna?

CAVARADOSSI

Lo giuro, amore! ... — Va!

TOSCA

Quanto mi affretti!

CAVARADOSSI

(con dolce rimprovero vedendo rispuntare la gelosia)
Ancora?

TOSCA

(cadendo nelle sue braccia e porgendogli la guancia)
No — perdona!

CAVARADOSSI

(sorridendo)
Davanti la Madonna?

TOSCA

È tanto buona!
(un bacio e Tosca esce correndo.)
(Appena uscita Tosca, Cavaradossi sta ascoltandone i passi allontanarsi, poi con precauzione socchiude l'uscio e guarda fuori. Visto tutto tranquillo, corre alla Cappella. Angelotti appare subito dietro la concellata.)

CAVARADOSSI

(aprendo la cancellata ad Angelotti, che naturalmente ha dovuto udire il dialogo precedente)
È buona la mia Tosca, ma credente;
al confessore nulla tien celato,
ond'io mi tacqui. È cosa più prudente.

ANGELOTTI

Siam soli?

CAVARADOSSI

Sì. Qual'è il vostro disegno?

ANGELOTTI

A norma degli eventi, uscir di Stato
o star celato in Roma. Mia sorella ...

CAVARADOSSI

L'Attavanti?

ANGELOTTI

Sì, ... ascose un muliebre
abbigliamento là sotto l'altare ...
vesti, velo, ventaglio. Appena imbruni
indosserò quei panni ...

CAVARADOSSI

Ora comprendo!
Quel fare circospetto
e il pregante fervore
in giovin donna e bella

Then you must promise, that goes without saying,
no lady is to join you,
no fair one and no dark one, not even praying.

CAVARADOSSI

That is a promise! Please!

TOSCA

Why do you rush me?

CAVARADOSSI *(with gentle reproach)*

You promised.

TOSCA

Yes, I know it.
(She falls into Cavaradossi's arms and offers him her cheek.)

CAVARADOSSI *(jokingly)*

Before the Holy Mother?

TOSCA *(moving her head towards the Madonna)*

She's so forgiving ... *(they embrace)*
(About to leave, she again looks at the picture and say maliciously:)
You'd better paint her eyes dark!
(Quick exit. Cavaradossi remains deep in thought. Remembering Angelotti, he makes sure that Tosca has left, opens the door and, seeing that everything is quiet, he runs over to the chapel. Angelotti appears behind the gate. Cavaradossi opens it and they shake hands affectionately.)

CAVARADOSSI

(To Angelotti, who, naturally, must have heard the preceding conversation:)
She's generous, my Tosca,
but she'll never hide a thought from her Father Confessor.
I did not tell her.
The less she knows, the better!

ANGELOTTI

The lady?

CAVARADOSSI

Gone. First tell me what you're planning.

ANGELOTTI

According to events, I'll leave the country,
or stay in Rome in hiding. Now my sister ...

CAVARADOSSI

L'Attavanti?

ANGELOTTI

Yes. She hid an entire lady's wardrobe
there, under the altar.
Mantle, bonnet, a fan, too!
(frightened, looks around)
Tonight I'll get away
disguised as a woman.

CAVARADOSSI

Now I see it!
I saw her for a moment here, she was kneeling and praying.
In one so young and lovely such fervor roused suspicion.

m'avean messo in sospetto
di qualche occulto amore!...
Era amor di sorella!

ANGELOTTI

Tutto ella ha osato
onde sottrarmi a Scarpia scellerato!

CAVARADOSSI

Scarpia?! Bigotto satiro che affina
colle devote pratiche — la foia
libertina — e strumento
al lascivo talento
fa il confessore e il boia!
Vi salverò, ne andasse della vita!
Ma indugiar fino a notte è mal sicuro.

ANGELOTTI

Temo del sole!

CAVARADOSSI

(indicando)
La cappella mette
ad un orto mal chiuso — indi un canneto
mena lungi pei campi a una mia villa.

ANGELOTTI

Mi è nota.

CAVARADOSSI

Ecco la chiave — innanzi sera
io vi raggiungo — portate con voi
le vesti femminili.

ANGELOTTI
(raccoglie in fascio le vestimenta sotto l'altare)
Ch'io le indossi?

CAVARADOSSI

Per or non monta, il sentiero è deserto.

ANGELOTTI

(per uscire)
Addio!

CAVARADOSSI

(accorrendo verso Angelotti)
Se urgesse il periglio, correte
al pozzo del giardin. L'acqua è nel fondo,
ma a mezzo della canna
un picciol varco
guida ad un antro oscuro,
rifugio impenetrabile e sicuro!
(un colpo di cannone; i due si guardano agitatissimi)

ANGELOTTI

Il cannon del castello!

CAVARADOSSI

Fu scoperta

I thought she was in love.
Now I see it. It was love for a brother!

ANGELOTTI

She'd stop at nothing to rescue me
from Scarpia and his agents.

CAVARADOSSI

Scarpia? . . . that lecherous hypocrite
who uses powers of State to satisfy his vilest inclinations,
and who uses, as tools for his purpose,
both hangman and confessor.
(with growing emotion) Whatever it may cost me, you shall be saved!
But to wait until nightfall is imprudent.

ANGELOTTI

Yes, but in daylight?

CAVARADOSSI

Right out there you'll find a door to a garden.
Look for a pathway through the suburbs
that leads you to my villa.

ANGELOTTI

I know it.

CAVARADOSSI

Here is the latch key.
I'll come and join you there this evening.
You must take along all the clothes your sister brought you.
(Angelotti picks up the bundle of clothes which his sister had hidden.)

ANGELOTTI

Shall I wear them?

CAVARADOSSI

You do not have to. You won't meet anybody.

ANGELOTTI *(about to leave)*

Till later.
(Cavaradossi rushes over to Angelotti.)

CAVARADOSSI

If there is any danger, you can take shelter in the well.
Deep down there's water
but halfway up the shaft
you will find a hiding place big enough to hold you.
If anything goes wrong, hide, as I told you.
(A cannon-shot is heard: the two friends look at each other in alarm.)

ANGELOTTI

That's the gun at the Fortress!

CAVARADOSSI

Your escape was discovered.

la fuga! Or Scarpia i suoi sbirri sguinzaglia!

ANGELOTTI

Addio!

CAVARADOSSI

(con subita risoluzione)
Con voi verrò. Staremo all'erta!

ANGELOTTI

Odo qualcun!

CAVARADOSSI

(con entusiasmo)
Se ci assalgon, battaglia!
(escono rapidamente dalla Cappella.)

SAGRESTANO

(entra correndo, tutto scalmanato, gridando)
Sommo giubilo, Eccellenza! . . .
(guarda verso l'impalcato e rimane sorpreso di non trovarvi neppure questa volta il pittore)
Non c'è più! Ne son dolente!
Chi contrista un miscredente
si guadagna un'indulgenza!
(accorono da ogni parte chierici, confratelli, allievi e cantori della Cappella. Tutti costoro entrano tumultuosamente)
Tutta qui la cantoria!
Presto! . . .
(altri allievi entrano in ritardo e alla fine si radunano tutti)

ALLIEVI

(colla massima confusione)
Dove?

SAGRESTANO

In sagrestia. *(spinge alcuni chierici)*

ALCUNI ALLIEVI

Ma che avvenne?

SAGRESTANO

Nol sapete?
Bonaparte . . . scellerato . . .
Bonaparte . . .

ALTRI ALLIEVI

Ebben? Che fu?

SAGRESTANO

Fu spennato, sfracellato
e piombato a Belzebù!

ALLIEVI, CANTORI, ECC.

Chi lo dice?
— È sogno!
— È fola!

Now Scarpia alerts all his agents!

ANGELOTTI

Till later . . .

CAVARADOSSI *(determined)*

I'll go with you. We'll stand together.

ANGELOTTI

I hear a step . . .

CAVARADOSSI *(enthusiastically)*

We will live to defeat them.
(They rush away through the chapel.)

SACRISTAN *(enters running, excited)*

What excitement, Excellency!
(greatly surprised that once again he doesn't find the painter)
He is gone. Now that's a pity!
If I irritate a pagan
I deserve a small indulgence.
All you choir boys, come in! Hurry!

CHOIR BOYS

(rushing in from all sides, in general confusion)
What for?

SACRISTAN

Come in, I tell you!
(urging them towards the Sacristy)

CHOIR BOYS

What has happened?

SACRISTAN

Don't you know yet? *(out of breath)* Bonaparte . . .
that old scoundrel . . . Bonaparte . . .

CHOIR BOYS

(surrounding the Sacristan, while others rush in and join them)
Go on! Do tell!

SACRISTAN

We attacked him and we sacked him,
and we sent him back to Hell!

CHOIR BOYS

And who says so? We don't believe it.

SACRISTAN

It's the truth, you can believe it.
I just heard the news, this moment.

CHOIR BOYS

There will be a celebration!

SAGRESTANO

E veridica parola
or ne giunse la notizia!
E questa sera
gran fiaccolata
veglia di gala a Palazzo Farnese,
ed un'apposita
nuova cantata
con Floria Tosca!
E nelle chiese
inni al Signore!
Presto a vestirvi,
non più clamore!

TUTTI

(ridendo e gridando gioiosamente)
Doppio soldo... *Te Deum*... Gloria!
Viva il Re!... Si festeggi la vittoria!
(Le loro grida e le loro risa sono al colmo, allorchè una voce ironica tronca bruscamente quella gazzara volgare di canti e risa. È Scarpia: dietro a lui Spoletta e alcuni sbirri)

SCARPIA

Un tal baccano in chiesa! Bel rispetto!

SAGRESTANO

(balbettando impaurito)
Eccellenza, il gran giubilo...

SCARPIA

Apprestate
per il *Te Deum*.
(tutti s'allontanano mogi: anche il Sagrestano fa per cavarsela, ma Scarpia bruscamente lo trattiene)
Tu resta!

SAGRESTANO

(impaurito)
Non mi muovo!

SCARPIA

(a Spoletta)
E tu va, fruga ogni angolo, raccogli
ogni traccia!

SPOLETTA

Sta bene!
(fa cenno a due sbirri di seguirlo)

SCARPIA

(ad altri sbirri)
Occhio alle porte,
ma senza dar sospetti!
(al Sagrestano) Ora a te. Pesa
le tue risposte. Un prigionier di Stato
pur or fuggito di Castel Sant'Angelo
s'è rifugiato qui.

SACRISTAN

Yes, we shall have a great celebration.
Scarpia is giving a gala reception,
and we shall hear, in a brand-new cantata,
Floria Tosca.
In all the churches people will pray.
Put on your vestments and stop the noise.
(loudly) Go . . . go . . . go and get dressed.

CHOIR BOYS

(Giggling, laughing and shouting gaily, paying no attention to the Sacristan, who tries in vain to push them towards the Sacristy.)
They'll pay double! Te Deum, gloria!
Long live the Queen!
There will be a celebration
and tonight we'll have a reception.
Te Deum, gloria!
There will be a victory feast!
(Scarpia appears unexpectedly and says, with great emphasis:)

SCARPIA

Is this a place of worship
or a madhouse?
(Seeing Scarpia they all stop in their tracks as though bewitched. The Sacristan stammers, dying with fear.)

SACRISTAN

Excellency, it's not every day . . .
(Scarpia is followed by Spoletta and other agents.)

SCARPIA

Go, get ready for the Te Deum.
(All slink away quietly; the Sacristan, too, hopes to disappear but Scarpia brusquely orders him to stay.)
You stay here.

SACRISTAN *(frightened, humbly)*

At your orders.

SCARPIA *(to Spoletta)*

And you there, take a few men with you
and search every corner!

SPOLETTA

At once, sir.

SCARPIA

(Orders two agents to follow him.)
Watch every exit.
(to the other agents, who do as they are told)
Don't attract attention!
(to the Sacristan)
Now for you! Think twice before you answer.
A traitor to his country
escaped this morning from the jail Sant'Angelo.
(with determination) I know that he is here!

SAGRESTANO
Misericordia!

SCARPIA
Forse c'è ancora. Dov'è la cappella
degli Attavanti?

SAGRESTANO
Eccola!
(*va al cancello e lo vede socchiuso*)
Aperta! Arcangeli!
E... un'altra chiave!

SCARPIA
Buon indizio. Entriamo.
(*entrano nella Cappella, poi ritornano: Scarpia, assai contrariato, ha fra le mani un ventaglio chiuso che agita nervosamente*)
Tardi! Fu grave sbaglio
quel colpo di cannone. Il mariolo
spiccato ha il volo, ma lasciò una presa...
preziosa — un ventaglio.
Qual complice il misfatto
preparò?
(*resta pensieroso, poi guarda attentamente il ventaglio; a un tratto egli vi scorge uno stemma*)
La marchesa
Attavanti!... Il suo stemma...
(*guarda intorno, scrutando ogni angolo della chiesa: i suoi occhi si arrestano sull'impalcato, sugli arnesi del pittore, sul quadro... e il noto viso dell'Attavanti gli appare riprodotto nel volto della santa*)
Il suo ritratto!
(*al Sagrestano*)
Chi fe' quelle pitture?

SAGRESTANO
Il cavaliere
Cavaradossi.

SCARPIA
Lui!
(*uno dei birri che seguì Scarpia, torna dalla Cappella portando il paniere che Cavaradossi diede ad Angelotti*)

SAGRESTANO
(*vedendolo*)
Numi! Il paniere!

SCARPIA
(*seguitando le sue riflessioni*)
Lui! L'amante di Tosca! Un uom sospetto!
Un volterrian!

SAGRESTANO
(*che andò a guardare il paniere*)
Vuoto? Vuoto!

SACRISTAN

Misericordia!

SCARPIA

But we shall find him.
Now which one is the Attavanti Chapel?

SACRISTAN

There it is.
(walks over to the gate, finding it ajar)
It's open! For goodness sakes!
This is not my key!

SCARPIA

That's suspicious. Let's enter.
(They enter the chapel but return at once. Scarpia, annoyed, holds a fan in his hands which he toys with nervously.)
(to himself) It was an error to have that cannon fired:
it only gave him a timely warning.
But he left me a keepsake . . . *(gesturing with the fan)*
the scoundrel left this fan here.
I wonder who the fair accomplice is!
(standing there thinking, closely scrutinizes the fan; suddenly discovers an emblem on it and cries out:)
The Marchessa Attavanti . . . it's her emblem.
(looks around, studying every corner of the church: his eyes are caught by the dais, the painter's tools and the painting . . . and by the well-known face of the Attavanti, which is seen on the painting, in the guise of a saint.)
This is her picture!
(to the Sacristan)
You know the man who did this?

SACRISTAN *(more and more frightened)*

A painter named Cavaradossi.

SCARPIA

He!

SACRISTAN

(discovers an agent coming out of the chapel with the basket)
Mercy, that's the basket.

SCARPIA *(continuing his trend of thought)*

He! The lover of Tosca!
A friend of traitors . . . perhaps a spy.

SACRISTAN

(After peering into the basket, he cries in great surprise.)
Empty, empty!

SCARPIA

Che hai detto?
(vede il birro col paniere)
Che fu?

SAGRESTANO

(prendendo il paniere)
Si ritrovò nella cappella
questo panier.

SCARPIA

Tu lo conosci?

SAGRESTANO

Certo!
(è esitante e pauroso)
È il cesto del pittor ... ma ... nondimeno ...

SCARPIA

Sputa quello che sai.

SAGRESTANO

Io lo lasciai ripieno
di cibo prelibato ...
il pranzo del pittore! ...

SCARPIA

(attento, inquirente per scoprir terreno)
Avrà pranzato!

SAGRESTANO

Nella cappella? Non ne avea la chiave
nè contava pranzar ... disse egli stesso.
Ond'io l'avea già messo
al riparo.
(mostra dove avea riposto il paniere e ve lo lascia)
(Libera me Domine)

SCARPIA

(Tutto è chiaro ...
la provvista — del sacrista
d'Angelotti fu la preda!)
(scorgendo Tosca che entra frettolosa)
Tosca? Che non mi veda.
(ripara dietro la colonna dov'è la pila dell'acqua benedetta)
(Per ridurre un geloso allo sbaraglio
Jago ebbe un fazzoletto — ed io un ventaglio!)

TOSCA

(corre al palco sicura di trovare Cavaradossi e sorpresa di non vederlo)
Mario?! Mario?!

SAGRESTANO

(che si trova ai piedi dell'impalcato)
Il pittore
Cavaradossi?
Chi sa dove sia

SCARPIA

(seeing the agent with the basket)
What is it? Speak up!

SACRISTAN

(taking the basket from the agent)
How did it get into the chapel?
I'd like to know.

SCARPIA

You know the basket?

SACRISTAN

Surely, I see it every day.
(stammers with fear)
But all the same I . . .

SCARPIA

Tell me all that you know.

SACRISTAN

(Still more frightened, almost crying, he shows him the empty basket.)
I always leave this basket
whenever he is painting.
It's just a bit of lunch.

SCARPIA *(continuing his inquiry to discover new clues)*
That means he ate here.

SACRISTAN

There in the Chapel? *(indicating "no" by a gesture)*
But how did he get in there?
And he wanted no food, that's what he told me.
Therefore I set it down here by the platform.
(showing where he left the basket and putting it there; impressed by the severe silence of Scarpia, mumbling to himself:)
Libera me, Domine!

SCARPIA *(to himself)*
I see it clearly; with the food the painter left untouched,
Angelotti stilled his hunger.
(Tosca returns in a state of great excitement: walks up to the dais and, not finding Cavaradossi, rushes all about the church looking for him. Scarpia, on seeing Tosca, quickly hides behind the column near the holy water basin, beckoning to the Sacristan to stay, who trembling approaches the painter's dais.)
Tosca? She mustn't see me.
If for Iago a handkerchief could do it,
maybe a lady's fan will work for Scarpia!

TOSCA

(Walking back to the dais, she cries out impatiently:)
Mario! Mario!

SACRISTAN *(walking up to her)*
If you want Cavaradossi, you're calling in vain.
He's here, and then before you look,

Sgattaiolò, svanì
per sua stregoneria. *(e se la svigna)*

TOSCA

Ingannata? No . . . no . . .
tradirmi egli non può!

SCARPIA

(ha girato la colonna e si presenta a Tosca, sorpresa del suo subito apparire. Intinge le dita nella pila e le offre l'acqua benedetta; fuori suonano le campane che invitano alla chiesa.)
Tosca divina
la mano mia
la vostra aspetta — piccola manina,
non per galanteria
ma per offrirvi l'acqua benedetta.

TOSCA

(tocca le dita di Scarpia e si fa il segno della croce)
Grazie, signor!
(Poco a poco entrano in chiesa, e vanno nella navata principale, popolani, borghesi, ciociare, trasteverine, soldati, pecorari, ciociari, mendicanti, ecc.: poi un Cardinale, col Capitolo, si reca all'altare maggiore; la folla, rivolta verso l'altare maggiore, si accalca nella navata principale.)

SCARPIA

Un nobile
esempio il vostro — al cielo
piena di santo zelo
attingete dell'arte il magistero
che la fede ravviva!

TOSCA

(distratta e pensosa)
Bontà vostra.

SCARPIA

Le pie donne son rare . . .
Voi calcate le scene . . .
(con intenzione)
ma in chiesa ci venite per pregare.

TOSCA

(sorpresa)
Che intendete?

SCARPIA

E non fate
Come certe sfrontate
che hanno di Maddalena *(indica il ritratto)*
viso e costumi . . . e vi trescan d'amore!

TOSCA

(scatta pronta)
Che? D'amore? Le prove!

SCARPIA

(mostra il ventaglio)
È arnese di pittore
questo?

he's gone again.
(hurries away)

TOSCA

He's deceived me? No, no, I know he's faithful to me.
(almost crying) I know that he is true!

SCARPIA *(with gentle insinuation)*

If I may linger and take your hand,
I won't caress you, only touch your finger,
not in a worldly spirit,
but offering holy water that will bless you.

TOSCA

(touches Scarpia's fingers and blesses herself)
You're very kind.

SCARPIA

I wish there were more as noble as you!
Your singing sets all the heavens ringing,
and your art, far from being vain and idle,
is an act of devotion.

TOSCA *(absent-mindedly)*

You're too generous.
(A few people are seen slowly entering the church.)

SCARPIA

But I know what I'm saying:
when on stage you are playing,
(with obvious intent)
but when you come to church, you come to pray.

TOSCA *(surprised)*

You're implying? . . .

SCARPIA

When you're kneeling you express what you're feeling.
(pointing to the painting)
Others, though they look like the Holy Madonna,
(making his meaning quite clear) really come to meet their lovers.

TOSCA *(wincing)*

What . . . what lovers? Suspicions! But prove it!

SCARPIA *(showing her the fan)*

Since when is this a tool of painters?

TOSCA

(lo afferra)
Un ventaglio? Dove
stava?

SCARPIA

Là su quel palco. Qualcun venne
certo a sturbar gli amanti
ed essa nel fuggir perdè le penne!

TOSCA

(esaminando il ventaglio)
La corona! Lo stemma! È l'Attavanti!
Ah presago sospetto!

SCARPIA

(Ho sortito l'effetto!)

TOSCA

(trattenendo a stento le lagrime, dimentica del luogo e di Scarpia)
Ed io venivo a lui tutta dogliosa
per dirgli: invan stassera
il ciel s'infosca
l'innamorata Tosca
dei regali tripudi è prigioniera!...

SCARPIA

(Già il veleno l'ha rosa.)
(mellifluo a Tosca)
O che v'offende,
dolce signora?
Una ribelle
lacrima scende
sovra le belle
guancie e le irrora;
dolce signora,
che mai v'accora?

TOSCA

Nulla!

SCARPIA

(insinuante)
Io darei la vita
per asciugar quel pianto.

TOSCA

(non ascoltandolo)
Io qui mi struggo e intanto
d'altra in braccio ei le mie smanie deride!

SCARPIA

(Morde il veleno.)

TOSCA

(sempre più crucciosa)
Dove son? Potessi
coglierli i traditori. Oh qual sospetto!

TOSCA *(grasping it)*
Let me see it. And where was it?
(Some peasants are seen entering.)

SCARPIA
Here by his scaffold.
Someone must have come to disturb the love birds.
The female flew away and lost some feathers.

TOSCA *(looking over the fan)*
L'Attavanti! Her emblem . . . The Attavanti!
Again that suspicion!

SCARPIA
I have made an impression.

TOSCA
(With great feeling, hardly able to hold back her tears, oblivious of Scarpia and of being in church.)
To think my poor deluded heart
was bleeding for fear that I might hurt him
if I told him tonight his loving Tosca would desert him . . .
would be forced by her duties to desert him . . .

SCARPIA
How my plan is succeeding.
(Shepherds and peasants are seen in the background.)
(in honeyed tones) What makes you tremble, most gracious lady?
You cannot hide the tears
that are stealing out of your eyes:
they simply won't let you, most gracious lady.
What has upset you?

TOSCA
Nothing!
(Some noblemen, accompanied by their ladies, enter the church.)
SCARPIA *(with emphasis)*
These bitter tears, I would give my life to dry them.
TOSCA *(not listening)*
Here I am, suffering and crying,
while he's laughing in the arms of another!

SCARPIA
Just as I planned it.
TOSCA *(very bitterly)*
If I knew!
(Some more citizens are sauntering in.)
But I will catch them yet both together!
(more and more upset) Ah, what a vision:
to find I'm right in that dreaded suspicion!
(in ever greater grief) I'm betrayed, I'm betrayed.
Our nest befouled by his cheating and lying.
(with a quick resolve)
But I will not allow it!

Ai doppi amori
è la villa ricetto.
Traditor, traditor
(con immenso dolore)
Oh mio bel nido insozzato di fango!
(con pronta risoluzione)
Vi piomberò inattesa.
(rivolta al quadro risoluzione)
Tu non l'avrai stanotte. Giuro!

SCARPIA

(scandolezzato, quasi rimproverandola)
In chiesa!

TOSCA

Dio mi perdona. Egli vede ch'io piango!
(parte in grande agitazione: Scarpia l'accompagna, fingendo di rassicurarla. Appena uscita Tosca, Scarpia ritorna presso la colonna e fa un cenno.)

SCARPIA

(a Spoletta che sbuca di dietro la colonna)
Tre sbirri ... Una carrozza. Presto — seguila
dovunque vada ... non visto ... e provvedi!

SPOLETTA

Sta bene. Il convegno?

SCARPIA

A Palazzo Farnese!
(Spoletta parte rapidamente con tre sbirri)
Va, Tosca! Nel tuo cuor s'annida Scarpia.
Va, Tosca. E Scarpia
che scioglie a volo il falco
della tua gelosia. Quanta promessa
nel tuo pronto sospetto! A doppia mira
tendo il voler, nè il capo del ribelle
è la più preziosa. Ah di quegli occhi
vittoriosi veder ... la fiamma
illanguidir con spasimo d'amore!
La doppia preda avrò. L'uno al capestro,
l'altra fra le mie braccia ...
(Il canto sacro dal fondo della chiesa lo scuote, come svegliandolo da un sogno. Si rimette, fa il segno della croce guardandosi intorno, e dice:)
Tosca, mi fai dimenticare Iddio!
(s'inginocchia e prega devotamente.)

(turns to the painting with a menacing gesture)
You'll never have your lover.
(with a desperate outcry)
I swear it!

SCARPIA *(shocked, as though reproaching her)*

Blaspheming?

TOSCA *(crying)*

God will forgive me when He sees how I'm crying.
(Crying bitterly. Scarpia offers his arm, sees her to the door, pretending to comfort her. After Tosca's departure, more and more people stream into the church. Scarpia, having accompanied Tosca, returns to the column; at his sign Spoletta appears suddenly. The crowd gathers in the background waiting for the Cardinal; some kneel and pray.)

SCARPIA

Spoletta, follow that lady. Hurry!
Do not arouse her suspicion . . . a carriage . . . be careful!

SPOLETTA

I shall be. Where'll I find you?

SCARPIA

Palazzo Farnese. *(Spoletta rushes off.)*
(with a sardonic smile) Go, Tosca!   Don't forget the name of Scarpia!
(The Cardinal, accompanied by the crowd, goes to the high altar. The Swiss guards keep the crowd in line.)
Go, Tosca! And Scarpia, remember, has been the one
who roused you to jealous passion.
All your suspicions are to me full of promise!
Don't forget the name of Scarpia!
(ironically)
Go, Tosca!
(Scarpia kneels and prays as the Cardinal passes. The Cardinal blesses the kneeling congregation.)
(ferociously) Mine is the power. Two-fold is my aim:
to see a traitor hanging
is by no means the greater one.
Soon I shall see her with her eyes all afire in passion;
(passionately excited) flaming delight,
her body trembling with love in my embraces!
Both of them shall be mine:
(wildly) one on the gallows,
and the other in Scarpia's arms!
(The entire congregation has turned towards the altar; some kneel. Scarpia stands motionless. He stares into thin air.)

SCARPIA *(as though awakening from a dream)*

Tosca!
For you I will forsake salvation.

CHORUS *(with religious zeal)*

Te aeternum Patrem omnis terra veneratur!
(The curtain falls quickly.)

ATTO SECONDO

La camera di Scarpia al piano superiore del Palazzo Farnese
(*Tavola imbandita. Un'ampia finestra verso il cortile del Palazzo. È notte.*)

SCARPIA

(*è seduto alla tavola e vi cena. Interrompe a tratti la cena per riflettere. Guarda l'orologio: è smanioso e pensieroso*)
Tosca è un buon falco!...
Certo a quest'ora
i miei segugi le due prede azzannano!
Doman sul palco
vedrà l'aurora
Angelotti e il bel Mario al laccio pendere.
(*suona — entra Sciarrone*)
Tosca è a palazzo?...

SCIARRONE

Un ciambellan ne usciva
pur ora in traccia

SCARPIA

(*accenna la finestra*)
Apri. — Tarda è la notte.
(*dal piano inferiore — ove la Regina di Napoli, Maria Carolina, dà una grande festa in onore di Melas — si ode il suonare di un'orchestra*)
Alla cantata ancor manca la Diva,
e strimpellan gavotte.
(*a Sciarrone*)
Tu attenderai la Tosca in sull'entrata;
le dirai ch'io l'aspetto
finita la cantata...
o meglio...
(*si alza e va a scrivere in fretta un biglietto*)
le darai questo biglietto.
(*Sciarrone esce*)

SCARPIA

(*siede ancora a tavola*)
Ella verrà... per amor del suo Mario!
Per amor del suo Mario al piacer mio
s'arrenderà. Tal dei profondi amori
è la profonda miseria. Ha più forte
sapore la conquista violenta
che il mellifluo consenso. Io di sospiri
e di lattiginose albe lunari
poco mi appago. Non so trarre accordi
di chitarra, nè oròscopo di fiori,
nè far l'occhio di pesce, o tubar come
tortora! (*alzandosi*)

ACT TWO

Scene: Palazzo Farnese.

(Scarpia's room; a table set for dinner, a large window facing the court of the palace. It is night.
Scarpia sits at the table and dines; occasionally interrupting his meal to ponder. He takes out his watch; his nervous attitude betrays a feverish anxiety.)

SCARPIA

Tosca's my falcon,
and I am certain that my hunters
will bring back a double prey.
Tomorrow morning, before the sunrise,
Angelotti and her Mario will be hanging high.
(He rings. Sciarrone enters.)
Tosca is not here yet?

SCIARRONE

One of your officers
has gone to fetch her.

SCARPIA *(to Sciarrone, pointing to the window)*

Open!
(The sound of an orchestra is heard from a lower floor, where the Queen is giving a party in honor of Melas.)
Night is advancing,
(to himself)
but the Cantata cannot start without Tosca.
They are scratching their fiddles.
(to Sciarrone)
Go down and wait for Tosca at the entrance.
Tell her I want to see her
as soon as she has finished . . .
(Sciarrone is about to leave) or better,
(Scarpia rises, goes to his desk, and hastily writes a note. Gives him the note)
here's a note that you will hand her. *(Sciarrone leaves.)*
(to himself)
I'm sure she'll come *(returns to the table and pours himself a glass of wine)*
out of love for her Mario.
Out of love for her Mario
she will surrender to my will.
There is no greater suffering
than the suffering that love brings.
Sweeter far are the raptures
of a violent conquest
than of willing surrender.
A lover sighing and pining
in the splendor of the moonlight isn't my fashion!
Not for me the poetry of sunsets, of midnight serenades.
(with disdain) I never ask a flower:
"Does she love me or love me not?"
(rises but stays close to the table)

Bramo. — La cosa bramata
persèguo, me ne sazio e via la getto
volto a nuova esca. Dio creò diverse
beltà e vini diversi. Io vo' gustare
quanto più posso dell'opra divina!
(beve)

SCIARRONE

(entrando)
Spoletta è giunto.

SCARPIA

Entri. In buon punto.
(si siede e tutt'occupato a cenare, interroga intanto Spoletta senza guardarlo)
O galantuomo, come andò la caccia?...

SPOLETTA

(Sant' Ignazio mi aiuta!)
Della signora seguimmo la traccia.
Giunti a un'erma villetta
tra le fratte perduta
ella vi entrò. Ne uscì sola ben presto.
Io allor scavalco lesto
il muro del giardin co' miei cagnotti
e piombo in casa...

SCARPIA

Quel bravo Spoletta!

SPOLETTA

(esitando)
Fiuto!... razzolo!... frugo!...

SCARPIA

(si avvede dell'indecisione di Spoletta e si leva ritto, pallido d'ira, le ciglia corrugate)
Ahi! l'Angelotti?...

SPOLETTA

Non s'è trovato.

SCARPIA

(furente)
Ah cane! Ah traditore!
Ceffo di basilisco,
alle forche!...

SPOLETTA

Gesù!
(cercando di scongiurare la collera di Scarpia)
Ciera il pittore...

SCARPIA

Cavaradossi?

SPOLETTA

(accenna di sì, ed aggiunge pronto)

Always I crave for the things that elude me.
Once I've had them I can discard them; on to stranger pleasures!
God created more than one wine, more than one beauty.
I want to taste all I can wring from the hand of the Maker.
(Sciarrone enters)

SCIARRONE

Spoletta's waiting.
(leaves to call Spoletta, who returns with him; Sciarrone remains by the door.)

SCARPIA *(very excited, yells)*

Splendid. Send him in here.
(Sitting down, he continues his meal while interrogating Spoletta without looking at him.)
Home is the hunter.
And where is the quarry?

SPOLETTA *(comes closer, frightened)*

(to himself) Saint Ignatius assist me!
Just as you ordered, we followed the lady
till she arrived at a villa, tucked away in a pine-grove.
First she went in, but returned in a moment.
I, with my agents, climbed the garden wall.
The rest of it was easy. And so we entered . . .

SCARPIA

My good old Spoletta!

SPOLETTA *(hesitates)*

. . . looking everywhere, searching.

SCARPIA

(Noticing Spoletta's hesitation he gets up, pale with fury, frowning.)
And Angelotti?

SPOLETTA

We couldn't find him.

SCARPIA

Not find him? Trying to cheat me!
Son of the devil's mother!
(shouting) I will hang you.

SPOLETTA *(trembling, trying to appease Scarpia)*

Oh Lord!
(timidly) But *he* was there.

SCARPIA *(interrupts him)*

Cavaradossi?

SPOLETTA *(nods "yes" but adds:)*

Ei sa
dove l'altro s'asconde. Ogni suo gesto
ogni accento, tradìa
tal beffarda ironia,
ch'io lo trassi in arresto!

SCARPIA

(con sospiro di soddisfazione)
Meno male!

SPOLETTA

(accena all'anticamera)
Egli è là.
(Scarpia passeggia meditando: a un tratto si arresta: dall'aperta finestra odesi la Cantata eseguita dai Cori nell sala della Regina.)

SCARPIA

(a Spoletta)
Introducete il Cavaliere. (Spoletta esce)
(a Sciarrone) A me
Roberti e il Giudice del Fisco.
(Sciarrone esce; Scarpia siede di nuovo.)
SPOLETTA e quattro sbirri introducono MARIO CAVARADOSSI. Poi ROBERTI, esecutore di Giustizia, il GIUDICE DEL FISCO con uno SCRIVANO e SCIARRONE.

CAVARADOSSI

(alteramente)
Tale violenza! . . .

SCARPIA

(con studiata cortesia)
Cavalier, vi piaccia
accomodarvi.

CAVARADOSSI

Vo' saper . . .

SCARPIA

(accennando una sedia al lato opposto della tavola)
Sedete.

CAVARADOSSI

(rifiutando)
Aspetto.

SCARPIA

E sia — Vi è noto che un prigione . . .
(odesi la voce di Tosca che prende parte alla Cantata)

CAVARADOSSI

La sua voce! . . .

SCARPIA

(che si era interrotto all'udire la voce di Tosca, riprende)
. . . vi è noto che un prigione
oggi è fuggito di Castel Sant' Angelo?

CAVARADOSSI

Ignoro.

SCARPIA

Eppur si pretende che voi

He knows where the other one's hiding;
but every gesture, every word that he spoke,
was so full of defiance that I had him arrested.

SCARPIA *(relieved)*

That is better.
(Paces the room; suddenly he stops. Through the open window one hears the Cantata performed in honor of the Queen. This means Tosca has arrived.)

SPOLETTA *(pointing to the anteroom)*

He's outside.

SCARPIA

(Suddenly struck by an idea, he says to Spoletta:)
Go, bring the gentleman in here. *(Spoletta leaves)*
(to Sciarrone)
I want Roberti, and ask the judge to see me.
*(Sits at the table again.
Spoletta, and three agents, bring in Cavaradossi; followed by Roberti, the torturer, a judge, a clerk and Sciarrone.)*

CAVARADOSSI

(rushing in, in great anger)
What an outrage!

SCARPIA *(with studied courtesy)*

Please sit down. I'm very glad to see you.

CAVARADOSSI

What's all this?

SCARPIA

(indicating a seat opposite him at the table)
Be seated.

CAVARADOSSI *(declining)*

I'm waiting.

SCARPIA

All right.
(staring at Cavaradossi before interrogating him)
You must have heard the story . . .

CAVARADOSSI

(Hearing Tosca's voice he exclaims, emotionally:)
That is Tosca!

SCARPIA

(He interrupts himself, also affected by Tosca's voice, but then continues his questioning.)
— the story of the man who bolted
this morning from Castel Sant'Angelo.

CAVARADOSSI

I have not.

SCARPIA

And yet I am told that

l'abbiate accolto in Sant'Andrea, provvisto
di cibo e vesti...

CAVARADOSSI

(risoluto)
Menzogna!

SCARPIA

(continuando a mantenersi calmo)
... e guidato
ad un vostro podere suburbano.

CAVARADOSSI

Nego. — Le prove?

SCARPIA

(mellifluo)
Un suddito fedele...

CAVARADOSSI

Al fatto. Chi mi accusa? I vostri sbirri
frugaron invan tutta la villa.

SCARPIA

Segno
che è ben celato

CAVARADOSSI

Sospetti di spia!

SPOLETTA

(offeso, interviene)
Alle nostre ricerche egli rideva...

CAVARADOSSI

E rido ancor.

SCARPIA

(con accento severo)
Questo è luogo di lacrime!
(si alza e chiude stizzito la finestra per non essere disturbato dai canti che hanno luogo nel piano sottostante: poi si volge imperioso a Cavaradossi:)
Ov'è Angelotti?

CAVARADOSSI

Non lo so.

SCARPIA

Negate
avergli dato cibo?

CAVARADOSSI

Nego!

SCARPIA

E vesti?

CAVARADOSSI

Nego!

SCARPIA

Ed asilo alla villa?

CAVARADOSSI

Nego!

you saw him this very day in Sant'Andrea;
supplied him with food and with clothing . . .

CAVARADOSSI *(with determination)*

They're lying.

SCARPIA *(remaining calm)*

. . . and allowed him to hide
in your villa in the suburbs.

CAVARADOSSI

Nonsense! Who says so?

SCARPIA

A very faithful servant.

CAVARADOSSI

That's nonsense. Who accused me?
(with irony) Your agents searched
but found my villa empty.

SCARPIA

That only proves you're clever.

CAVARADOSSI

All spies are suspicious.

SPOLETTA *(breaks in, offended)*

Every question we asked
he answered with laughter.

CAVARADOSSI

And still I laugh.

SCARPIA *(terrifying in his anger)*

I think tears more appropriate!
(threatening) I warn you *(nervously)* the last time.
You will answer.
(*Irritated and disturbed by the voices of the Cantata, he closes the window.*)
(imperiously) Where's Angelotti?

CAVARADOSSI

I don't know.

SCARPIA

I ask, is it true that you have fed him?

CAVARADOSSI

Never.

SCARPIA

Disguised him?

CAVARADOSSI

Never.

SCARPIA

Received him in your villa,
where right now he's hiding?

CAVARADOSSI *(emphatically)*

Never, never!

SCARPIA

E che là sia nascosto?

CAVARADOSSI

(con forza)
Nego! nego!

SCARPIA

(astutamente, ritornando calmo)
Via, Cavaliere, riflettete: saggia non è
cotesta ostinatezza vostra. Angoscia
grande, pronta confessione eviterà. Io vi
consiglio dite, dov'è dunque Angelotti?

CAVARADOSSI

Non lo so.

SPOLETTA

(O bei tratti di corda!)

Tosca, *entra affannosa*

SCARPIA

(vedendo Tosca)
Eccola!)

TOSCA

(vede Cavaradossi e corre ad abbracciarlo)
Mario,
tu qui?!

CAVARADOSSI

(sommessamente)
(Di quanto là vedesti, taci,
o m'uccidi!...)
(Tosca accenna che ha capito)

SCARPIA

(con solennità)
Mario Cavaradossi,
qual testimonio il Giudice vi aspetta.
(a Roberti)
Pria le forme ordinarie. — Indi... a miei cenni.
(Sciarrone apre l'uscio che dà alla camera della tortura. Il Giudice vi entra e gli altri lo seguono, rimanendo Tosca e Scarpia. Spoletta si ritira presso alla porta in fondo alla sala)

SCARPIA

Ed or fra noi parliamo da buoni amici. Via
quell'aria sgomenta... *(accenna a Tosca di sedere)*

TOSCA

(siede con calma studiata)
Sgomento alcun non ho.

SCARPIA

La storia del ventaglio?...
(passa dietro al canapè su quale si è seduta Tosca e vi si appoggia, parlando sempre con galanteria)

SCARPIA *(remaining calm, almost paternal)*
May I suggest you think it over?
Nothing is to be gained by your remaining stubborn.
You will regret it
if you don't confess your evil deeds.
Let me advise you: speak up.
Tell me, where's Angelotti?

CAVARADOSSI
I don't know.

SCARPIA
I ask you for the last time ...
where is he?

CAVARADOSSI
Don't know.

SPOLETTA
He is asking for trouble.

SCARPIA
(Tosca enters, alarmed: seeing Cavaradossi, she runs towards him and embraces him.)
Here she is.

TOSCA
Mario, you here?

CAVARADOSSI *(whispers to Tosca, who indicates that she understands)*
Don't say a word of what you saw there,
if you love me.

SCARPIA
Mario Cavaradossi, this worthy judge
will take your deposition.
(motions to Sciarrone to open the door to the torture chamber)
(turning to Roberti) Try the usual procedure. Later I'll instruct you.
(The judge enters the torture chamber: the others follow him, leaving Tosca and Scarpia behind; Spoletta withdraws to the door at the back of the room. Sciarrone closes the door. Tosca shows surprise; Scarpia reassures her, being elaborately gentle with her.)
(with gallantry) Now you and I can have a word in friendship.
(asking Tosca to sit down)
No more sorrow on that lovely face?

TOSCA
(sits down, pretending calm)
I don't know what you mean.

SCARPIA
(Passes behind the sofa where Tosca sits and leans against it.)
The fan that we discovered ...

TOSCA
(con simulata indifferenza)
Fu sciocca gelosia.

SCARPIA
L'Attavanti non era dunque alla villa?

TOSCA
No:
egli era solo.

SCARPIA
Solo? — Ne siete ben sicura?

TOSCA
Nulla sfugge ai gelosi. Solo! solo!

SCARPIA
(prende una sedia, la porta di fronte a Tosca, vi si siede e guarda fissamente Tosca)
Davver?

TOSCA
(irritata)
Solo! si!

SCARPIA
Quanto fuoco! Par che abbiate paura
di tradirvi.
(chiamando) Sciarrone: che dice il Cavalier?

SCIARRONE
(apparendo sul limitare dell'uscio)
Nega.

SCARPIA
(a voce più alta verso l'uscio aperto)
Insistiamo.
(Sciarrone rientra nella camera di tortura, chiudendone l'uscio)

TOSCA
(ridendo)
Oh, inutile.

SCARPIA
(serissimo, si alza e passeggia)
Lo vedremo, signora.

TOSCA
Dunque per compiacervi si dovrebbe mentir?

SCARPIA
No; ma il vero potrebbe abbreviargli un'ora
assai penosa...

TOSCA
(sorpresa)
Un'ora penosa? Che vuol dir?
Che avviene in quella stanza?

SCARPIA
È forza che si adempia
la legge.

TOSCA
Oh! Dio!... che avviene?

TOSCA *(with simulated indifference)*

I'm not a jealous woman.

SCARPIA

Do you mean that you didn't find L'Attavanti?

TOSCA

No. No one was with him.

SCARPIA

Really? *(inquiring maliciously)* How can you be so certain?
(Puts a chair in front of Tosca; staring at her, he sits down.)

TOSCA

Jealous eyes are the sharpest. *(annoyed, insisting)* There was no one.

SCARPIA *(irritated)*

Indeed!

TOSCA

No one, no!

SCARPIA

What an outburst!
One could almost believe that you are frightened.
(turning towards the door of the torture chamber, he shouts:)
Sciarrone, what does our witness say?

SCIARRONE

(appearing at the door)
Nothing.

SCARPIA *(louder)*

Let's continue.
(Sciarrone goes back, closing the door.)

TOSCA *(laughing)*

Oh, it's useless.

SCARPIA *(rises, paces about the room; seriously)*

We shall find out, Signora.

TOSCA *(slowly, with an ironic smile)*

Maybe you'd like it better
if I told you a lie?

SCARPIA

No, but telling the truth
might avoid some most unpleasant moments.

TOSCA *(astonished)*

Some unpleasant moments?
In what way?
What's happening to Mario?

SCARPIA

There is a law and I shall enforce it.

TOSCA

Oh God, what law? Go on! Go on!

SCARPIA

Legato mani e piè
il vostro amante ha un cerchio uncinato alle tempia,
che a ogni niego ne sprizza sangue senza mercè.

TOSCA

(balza in piedi)
Non è ver, non è vero! Sogghigno di demòne...
Quale orrendo silenzio!... Ah! un gemito... pietà...
(ascolta ansiosamente)

SCARPIA

Sta in voi salvarlo.

TOSCA

Ebbene... ma cessate!

SCARPIA

(va presso all'uscio)
Sciarrone,
sciogliete.

SCIARRONE

(si presenta sul limitare)
Tutto?

SCARPIA

Tutto.
(Sciarrone entra di nuovo nella camera della tortura, chiudendo)
(a Tosca) Ed or... la verità.

TOSCA

Ch'io lo veda!...

SCARPIA

No!

TOSCA

(riesce ad avvicinarsi all'uscio)
Mario!

LA VOCE DI CAVARADOSSI

Tosca!

TOSCA

Ti fanno male
ancora?

LA VOCE DI CAVARADOSSI

No — coraggio — Taci — Sprezzo il dolor.

SCARPIA

(avvicinandosi a Tosca)
Orsù, Tosca, parlate.

TOSCA

(rinfrancata dalle parole di Cavaradossi)
Non so nulla!

SCARPIA

Non vale
la prova?... Ripigliamo...

TOSCA

(si frappone fra l'uscio e Scarpia, per impedire che dia l'ordine)

SCARPIA *(with increasing vehemence)*
They've tied him hand and foot,
and they have laid a steel-pointed ring over his temples.
For every question he does not answer he pays in blood.

TOSCA
(jumping up)
Oh no, oh no. Contemptible torturer!
(She listens in great anxiety, her hands clutching the back of the sofa.)

CAVARADOSSI *(a long moan)*
Ah.

TOSCA
How horrible! Enough, enough.

SCARPIA
It's your decision.

TOSCA
All right, but release him, release him!

SCARPIA
(opens the door to the torture chamber)
Sciarrone, enough now.

SCIARRONE
(appearing at the door)
Stop it?

SCARPIA
Stop it!
(returning to the torture chamber, Sciarrone closes the door)
I want to hear the truth.

TOSCA
Let me see him.

SCARPIA
No.

TOSCA
(has succeeded in getting close to the door)
Mario.

CAVARADOSSI *(in pain)*
(in the torture chamber) Tosca!

TOSCA
They still make you suffer?

CAVARADOSSI
No, it's nothing. Courage, courage! I laugh at pain.

SCARPIA
(walking towards Tosca)
And now, Tosca, I'm waiting.

TOSCA *(with conviction)*
I know nothing.

SCARPIA
You don't believe I mean it?
(trying to go to the door) Roberti, let's continue.

TOSCA
No! I beg you!

Fermate!...no...che orror!

SCARPIA

Parlate!...

TOSCA

No...mostro!
lo strazi...l'uccidi!

SCARPIA

Lo strazia quel vostro
silenzio assai più.

TOSCA

Tu ridi...tu ridi
all'orrida pena?

SCARPIA

(con feroce ironia)
Mai Tosca alla scena
più tragica fu.
(con fermezza a Tosca, guardandola fissa negli occhi)
Qui pianti e rimbrotti
son vani.

TOSCA

(supplichevole)
Mercè!

SCARPIA

Ov'è l'Angelotti?
Rispondi, dov'è?

TOSCA

(con voce soffocata)
Nol so.

SCARPIA

La vendetta
su Mario cadrà.
(grida in tono di comando)
Sciarrone!

TOSCA

(smarrita)
No...aspetta...
(vuol parlare, smania, resiste ancora)
Non posso...
(a mani giunte)
Pietà...

SCARPIA

(per finirla)
Aprite le porte
che n'oda i lamenti.
(Spoletta apre l'uscio e sta ritto sulla soglia)

LA VOCE DI CAVARADOSSI

Vi sfido.

SCARPIA

(imperioso)
Più forte.

(Standing between the door and Scarpia; trying to prevent him from giving his order.)

SCARPIA

All right, I'm waiting.

TOSCA

No, no. You're a monster.
How you hate him, you monster.
You hate him, you'll kill him!

SCARPIA

Oh no, it's not Scarpia who'll kill him!
It's your silence!
(laughs)

TOSCA

You're laughing? You laugh at his suffering.

SCARPIA *(admiringly)*

You've never yet played a more tragical role.
(Tosca, terrified, walks away from Scarpia who, in a sudden outburst of ferocity, turns to Spoletta.)
(shouting) Let's open the doors
so we'll hear how he's screaming.
(Spoletta opens the door and remains standing there.)

CAVARADOSSI *(in the torture chamber)*

I defy you . . .

SCARPIA *(shouting to Roberti)*

Still harder, still harder.

CAVARADOSSI

. . . defy you.

SCARPIA *(to Tosca)*

Now tell me.

TOSCA

I cannot.

SCARPIA

Where is he?

TOSCA

Ah, I know nothing.
(desperately) Ah, what can I do?

SCARPIA *(insists)*

Speak, where is Angelotti?

TOSCA

No, no!

SCARPIA

That's all I ask. Tell me where did he go to hide?
It's time you told me. Speak up!

TOSCA
È troppo matrir!
(si rivolge ancora supplichevole a Scarpia, il quale fa cenno a Spoletta di lasciare avvicinare Tosca: questa va presso all'uscio aperto ed esterrefatta alla vista dell'orribile scena, si rivolge a Cavaradossi col massimo dolore:)
O Mario, consenti
ch'io parli?...

LA VOCE DI CAVARADOSSI
No.

TOSCA
(con insistenza)
Ascolta,
non posso più...

LA VOCE DI CAVARADOSSI
Stolta,
che sai?... che puoi dir?...

SCARPIA
(irritatissimo per le parole di Cavaradossi e temendo che da questa Tosca sia ancora incoraggiata a tacere, grida terribile a Spoletta:)
Ma fatelo tacere!...
(Spoletta enta nella camera della tortura e n'esce poco dopo, mentre Tosca, vinta dalla terribile commozione, cade prostrata sul canapè e con voce singhiozzante si rivolge a Scarpia che sta impassibile e silenzioso. Intanto Spoletta brontola preghiere sottovoce.)

TOSCA
Io... son io
che così torturate!... Torturate
l'anima...
(scoppia in singhiozzi strazianti, mormorando:)
Sì, mi torturate l'anima!
(Scarpia, profittando dell'accasciamento di Tosca, va presso la camera della tortura e fa cenno di ricominciare il supplizio — un grido orribile si fa udire — Tosca si alza di scatto e subito con voce soffocata dice rapidamente a Scarpia:)
nel pozzo... nel giardino...

SCARPIA
Là è l'Angelotti?

TOSCA
Sì...

SCARPIA
(forte, verso la camera della tortura)
Basta, Roberti.

SCARPIA
(che ha aperto l'uscio) È svenuto!

TOSCA
(a Scarpia) Assassino!...
Voglio vederlo...

SCARPIA
Portatelo qui.
(Sciarrone rientra e subito appare Cavaradossi svenuto, portato dagli sbirri che lo depongono sul canapè. Tosca corre a lui, ma l'orrore della vista dell'amante

TOSCA

Ah . . . ah, I can't bear it.
Ah, this is too much to bear.
(Beseeches Scarpia, who motions to Spoletta to let Tosca approach the door: she does so, and horrified by the terrible scene, turns towards Cavaradossi. Cavaradossi cries out.)

TOSCA *(aggrieved)*

Mario . . . allow me to tell him!

CAVARADOSSI *(in a broken voice)*

No, no.

TOSCA

I beg you. This is too much.

CAVARADOSSI

Tell him? You can't. You don't know.

SCARPIA

(Irritated by Cavaradossi's words, fearing that they might further encourage Tosca to keep silent, he yells to Spoletta.)
I want him to be silenced.
(Spoletta enters the chamber but soon returns. Tosca, overcome by horror, falls on the sofa and turns, sobbing, to Scarpia, who remains impassible and silent.)

TOSCA

Tell me why you hate me so.
You know that it is *me* whom you torture!
In *his* flesh you torture *me*.
(bursting into wild sobs)
Yes, torture me . . . tearing my heart out!
*(Scarpia, making the most of Tosca's despair, goes to the door and orders the torture to be continued. Cavaradossi groans.
Hearing his cry, Tosca suddenly rises and says to Scarpia, in a quick whisper:)*
The well . . . in the garden . . .

SCARPIA

That's where he is hiding?

TOSCA *(stifling)*

Yes.

SCARPIA *(shouts towards the torture chamber)*

That's all, Roberti.

SCIARRONE *(in the door)*

He has fainted.

TOSCA *(to Scarpia)*

Bloody murderer. I want to see him.

SCARPIA *(to Sciarrone)*

You may bring him in.
(Cavaradossi is brought in by the agents who put him on the sofa: he has fainted. Tosca rushes over to him but is terrified to see him bleeding profusely; she covers

insanguinato è cosi forte, ch'essa sgomentata si copre il volto per non vederlo — poi, vergognosa di questa sua debolezza, si inginocchia presso di lui, baciandolo e piangendo. — Sciarrone, il Giudice, Roberti, lo Scrivano escono dal fondo, mentre, ad un cenno di Scarpia, Spoletta ed gli sbirri fermano.)

CAVARADOSSI
(riavendosi)
Floria!...

TOSCA
(coprendolo di baci)
Amore...

CAVARADOSSI
Sei tu?...

TOSCA
Quanto hai penato
anima mia! Ma il giusto
iddio lo punirà!

CAVARADOSSI
Tosca, hai parlato?

TOSCA
No, amor...

CAVARADOSSI
Davver?...

SCARPIA
(forte, a Spoletta)
Nel pozzo
del giardin. — Va, Spoletta.
(Spoletta esce: Cavaradossi, che ha udito, si leva minaccioso contro Tosca; poi le forze l'abbandonano e si lascia cadere sul canapè, esclamando con rimprovero pieno e amarezza verso Tosca:)

CAVARADOSSI
Ah! m'hai tradito!...

TOSCA
(supplichevole)
Mario!

CAVARADOSSI
(respingendo Tosca che si abbraccia stretta a lui)
Maledetta!
(Sciarrone, a un tratto, irrompe tutto affannoso)

SCIARRONE
Eccellenza... ah, quali nuove!...

SCARPIA
(sorpreso)
Che vuol dir quel'aria afflitta?

SCIARRONE
Un messaggio di sconfitta...

SCARPIA
Qual sconfitta? Come? Dove?

SCIARRONE
A Marengo...

her eyes with her hands. Ashamed of her weakness, she approaches him; covering him with her kisses and tears. Sciarrone, the judge, Roberti, and the clerk exit; at a sign from Scarpia, Spoletta and the agents remain.)

CAVARADOSSI *(coming to)*

Floria!

TOSCA

My darling!

CAVARADOSSI

My love!

TOSCA *(warmly)*

How you have suffered, Mario, my love.
But he will answer before the Lord.

CAVARADOSSI

Tosca, did you tell him?

TOSCA

No, my love.

CAVARADOSSI

You're certain?

TOSCA

Yes.

SCARPIA *(to Spoletta, with authority)*

He's hiding in the garden well . . . Spoletta.

CAVARADOSSI *(rises, threatening Tosca)*

You've betrayed me! *(falls back, broken)*

TOSCA *(embracing Cavaradossi)*

Mario!

CAVARADOSSI *(trying to repel her)*

You've betrayed me!

TOSCA

Mario!

SCIARRONE

(enters in alarm)
Excellency, this is dreadful.

SCARPIA *(surprised)*

You are trembling. What's the matter?

SCIARRONE

I have news of a disaster.

SCARPIA

A disaster? What can that be?

SCIARRONE

At Marengo . . .

SCARPIA *(shouts impatiently)*

At Marengo?

SCARPIA
(impaziente)
Tartaruga!

SCIARRONE
Bonaparte è vincitor...

SCARPIA
Melas!

SCIARRONE
No. Melas è in fuga!...
(Cavaradossi, che con ansia crescente ha udito le parole di Sciarrone, trova nel proprio entusiasmo la forza di alzarsi minaccioso in faccia a Scarpia)

CAVARADOSSI
Vittoria! Vittoria!!
L'alba vindice appar
che fa gli empi tremar!
Libertà sorge crollano
tirannidi!
Del sofferto martir
me vedrai qui gioir...
il tuo cuor trema, o Scarpia.
carnefice!
(Tosca, disperatamente aggrappandosi a Cavaradossi, tenta, con parole interrotte, di farlo tacere, mentre Scarpia risponde a Cavaradossi con sarcastico sorriso:)

SCARPIA
Braveggia, urla! — T'affretta
a palesarmi il fondo
dell'alma ria!
Va! — Moribondo,
il capestro t'aspetta!
(ed irritato per le parole di Cavaradossi, grida agli sbirri:)
Portatemelo via!
(Sciarrone e gli sbirri s'impossessano di Cavaradossi, e lo trascinano verso la porta. Tosca con un supremo sforzo tenta di tenersi stretta a Cavaradossi, ma invano: essa è brutalmente respinta)

TOSCA
Mario... con te...
(gli sbirri conducono via Cavaradossi; li seguono Spoletta e Sciarrone: Tosca si avventa per seguir Cavaradossi, ma Scarpia si colloca innanzi la porta e la chiude, respingendo Tosca)

SCARPIA
Voi no!

TOSCA
(con un gemito)
Salvatelo!

SCARPIA
Io?... Voi!
(si avvicina alla tavola, vede la sua cena lasciata a mezzo e ritorna calmo e sorridente)

SCIARRONE

Bonaparte won the battle.

SCARPIA

Our troops?

SCIARRONE

No, our troops were beaten.
(Cavaradossi, who has heard Sciarrone's words with increasing anxiety, finds in his returning enthusiasm the strength to get up and threaten Scarpia to his face.)

CAVARADOSSI *(enthusiastically)*

Victorious! Victorious!
Freedom's bugles call. Tyrants tremble and fall,
and united we cry: Down with all tyranny.
All our anguish and pain was not suffered in vain.
Fear is striking the breast of Scarpia, the murderer!
You murderer, you murderer!

TOSCA

(In despair, throws her arms around Cavaradossi, trying to calm him.)
Mario, Mario, do think of *me*.
You're mad, Mario!
(to Scarpia) You must not listen!
He's mad, he's mad! Forgive him, please!
I go with you ... no ... no!

SCARPIA *(with a cynical glance at Cavaradossi)*

I like him ranting and prating;
it only shows his soul in its abject blackness!
Go to your scaffold where the hangman is waiting.
Go, go!
(irritated by Cavaradossi's words, orders the agents:)
Remove him from my sight!
(Sciarrone and the agents seize Cavaradossi and drag him towards the door.)
Go to your scaffold, go, go!

TOSCA

(trying to resist them)
Ah, Mario, Mario.
(clinging to Cavaradossi, still trying to resist the agents)
My love, my love.
(trying to pass Scarpia)

SCARPIA

(holding Tosca back, he closes the door)
You stay!

TOSCA *(with a moan)*

Be generous.

SCARPIA

I? You!
(Returning to the table, he looks at his interrupted meal; calmly and with a smile)

La povera mia cena fu interrotta.
(vedendo Tosca abbattuta, immobile, ancora presso la porta)
Così accasciata?... Via, bella signora
sedete qui. — Volete che cerchiamo
insieme il modo di salvarlo?
(Tosca si scuote e lo guarda: Scarpia sorride sempre e si siede, accennando in pari tempo di sedere a Tosca)
E allor sedete... e favelliamo... E intanto
un sorso. È vin di Spagna...
(riempie il bicchiere e lo porge a Tosca)
Un sorso
per rincorarvi.

TOSCA

(fissando sempre Scarpia si avvicina lentamente alla tavola, siede risoluta di fronte a Scarpia, poi coll'accento del più profondo disprezzo gli chiede:)
Quanto?

SCARPIA

(imperturbabile, versandosi da bere)
Quanto?... *(ride)*

TOSCA

Il prezzo!...

SCARPIA

Già. — Mi dicon venal, ma a donna bella
io non mi vendo a prezzo di moneta.
Se la giurata fede
devo tradir, ne voglio altra mercede.
Quest'ora io l'attendeva.
Già mi struggea
l'amore della diva!...
Ma poc'anzi ti mirai
qual non ti vidi mai!
Quel tuo pianto era lava
ai sensi miei — ed il tuo sguardo,
che odio in me dardeggiava,
mie brame inferociva!...
Agil qual leopardo
ti avvinghiasti all'amante — in quell'istante
io t'ho giurata mia!...
Mia!...
(si leva, stendendo le braccia verso Tosca: questa, che aveva ascoltato immobile, impietrita, le lascive parole di Scarpia, s'alza di scatto e si rifugia dietro il canapè)

TOSCA

Tu?...

SCARPIA

Sì, e t'avrò!

TOSCA

(correndo alla finestra)
Piuttosto giù mi avvento!

SCARPIA

(freddamente)

My modest little meal was interrupted.
(He sees Tosca, who stands by the door motionless and downcast.)
You seem disheartened?
Come, my lovely Signora,
sit down with me.
Perhaps together we can find
a way to save your Mario? We might!
(sits down, inviting Tosca to do the same)
Sit down here, let's talk it over.
(He polishes a glass with his napkin and then lifts it up to the candle, inspecting it.)
And in the meantime, a glass of sherry.
(gently) Believe me, it will revive you.

TOSCA

(Sits opposite Scarpia and stares at him; with her elbows on the table, resting her head on her hands, she says to Scarpia with profound contempt:)
How much?

SCARPIA

How much?

TOSCA

... to bribe you?
(Scarpia laughs)

SCARPIA

Yes, I know what they say: that I can be bought.
But I'm not for sale to lovely ladies
for something cheap as money. No, no!
(making his intention clear)
No lovely lady can ever buy me with something cheap as money.
If I am asked to break the oath that I swore,
(very outspoken)
I want a higher payment. I want a much higher payment.
Tonight's the night I've longed for!
Since first I saw you desire has consumed me,
but tonight, though you hope to defy me, you can no more deny me.
(rises in great emotion) When you cried out, despairing, passion inflamed me,
and your glances almost drove beyond bearing
the lust to which you've doomed me.
How your hatred enhances my resolve to possess you!
I may curse or bless you, but you must be mine!
(approaches Tosca, opening his arms)
You are mine!
(Tosca, horrified, runs to the window)

TOSCA *(pointing to the window)*

Ah, I'd rather take my life first.

SCARPIA

But how about your darling Mario?

In pegno
il tuo Mario mi resta!...

TOSCA

Ah! Miserable
L'orribile mercato!...
(*corre verso la porta*)

SCARPIA

(*ironico*)
Violenza non ti farò sei libera. Va pure.
Ma è fallace speranza: la Regina
farebbe solo grazia ad un cadavere!
(*Tosca retrocede spaventata, e fissando Scarpia si lascia cadere sul canapè; poi stacca gli occhi da Scarpia con un gesto di supremo disgusto e di odio*)
Come tu m'odii!

TOSCA

Ah! Dio!...

SCARPIA

(*avvicinandosele*)
Così ti voglio!

TOSCA

(*con ribrezzo*)
Non toccarmi — demonio — t'odio, t'odio,
abbietto, vile!
(*fugge da Scarpia inorridita*)

SCARPIA

Che importa? Sei mia...
Spasimi d'ira e spasimi d'amore!

TOSCA

Vile!!

SCARPIA

Mia!! (*cerca di afferrarla*)

TOSCA

(*inseguendola*)
Mia...

TOSCA

No — aiuto!
(*un lontano rullo di tamburi a poco a poco si avvicina poi si dilegua lontano*)

SCARPIA

(*fermandosi*)
L'odi?
E il tamburo. S'avvia. Guida la scorta
ultima ai condannati. Il tempo passa!
(*Tosca, dopo aver ascoltato con ansia terribile, si allontana dalla finestra e si appoggia, estenuata, al canapè*)

TOSCA

How do you dare to offer me such a bargain?
(She rushes to the door, intending to appeal to the Queen.)

SCARPIA

(Guessing her secret thought, he lets her pass.)
You're free to do as you please. You want to leave?
You're free to.
(Tosca, crying out with relief, is about to exit; Scarpia detains her with a gesture, smiling ironically.)
But your Queen cannot save him.
Who can pardon a man who's swinging from the hangman's noose?
(convinced and pleased) How you detest me!
(Tosca draws back in horror and lets herself fall on the sofa; then withdraws her eyes from Scarpia with a gesture of supreme contempt and hatred.)

TOSCA *(full of hatred and contempt)*

I do!

SCARPIA

(approaching her)
And that's the way I want you!

TOSCA *(in exasperation)*

Do not touch me, you murderer! *(fleeing Scarpia in horror)*
How I hate you, you coward, murderer!

SCARPIA

Detest me! *(coming still closer)*
Passionate in hating, passionate in loving.

TOSCA

Monster!

SCARPIA

(trying to seize her)
Tosca!

TOSCA

(behind the table)
Murderer. I hate you!
(A drum roll is heard, slowly approaching. At the sound, both stand motionless.)

SCARPIA *(with emphasis)*

Listen, hear the drum roll. You hear it?
This is the drum announcing an execution!
There's not much time left.
(Tosca, having listened with great anxiety, leaves the window and leans against the sofa, exhausted.)

Sai quale oscura opra laggiù si compia?
Là si drizza un patibolo. Al tuo Mario,
per tuo voler, non resta che un'ora di vita.
(freddamente si appoggia ad un angolo della tavola continuando a guardare Tosca)

TOSCA

(nel massimo dolore)
Vissi d'arte, vissi d'amore, non feci mai
male ad anima viva!
Con man furtiva
quante miserie conobbi, alleviai.
Sempre con fè sincera
la mia preghiera
ai santi tabernacoli salì.
Diedi fiori agli altar, diedi gioielli
della Madonna al manto,
e diedi il canto
agli astri, al ciel, che ne ridean più belli.
Nell'ora del dolore
perchè, Signore,
perchè me ne rimuneri così?

SCARPIA

(avvicinandosi di nuovo a Tosca)
Risolvi?

TOSCA

Mi vuoi supplice a tuoi piedi?
(inginocchiandosi innanzi a Scarpia)
Ecco — vedi —
le man giunte io stendo a te!
E mercè,
umiliata e vinta, aspetto
d'un tuo detto.

SCARPIA

Sei troppo bella, Tosca, e troppo amante.
Cedo. — A misero prezzo
tu, a me una vita, io, a te chieggo un istante!

TOSCA

(alzandosi, con senso di gran disprezzo)
Va — va — mi fai ribrezzo!
(bussano alla porta)

SCARPIA

Chi è là?

SPOLETTA

(entrando trafelato)
Eccellenza, l'Angelotti al nostro
giunger si uccise.

SCARPIA

Ebbene lo si appenda
morto alle forche. E l'altro prigioniero?

Tell me: do you really know what is going on there?
No? They're hoisting the gallows there,
(Tosca makes a movement of frightened despair.)
and your Mario, whom you have doomed,
will not see the sun of tomorrow.
(Tosca, overcome with grief, falls back on the sofa. Scarpia, unimpressed, stands by the supper table, pours himself some coffee and drinks it, looking at Tosca all the while.)

TOSCA

Love for beauty, love and compassion . . .
they gave to my art its true inspiration.
Sweet consolation I brought to those who are poor and unhappy.
Always with deep emotion, my true devotion
I poured out to the glory of the Lord.
I brought with deep devotion
flowers to adorn His house.
Despairing of tomorrow, my head is bowed in sorrow.
Oh why, my Lord, withdraw Your hand from me?
My worldly treasure I gladly laid on His altar;
I'd never falter in singing of His greatness without measure.
If love is doomed to die,
Oh Lord, my Lord, tell me — why? Ah,
Lord, why do You withdraw Your hand from me?
(sobbing)

SCARPIA

Your answer?

TOSCA

(kneeling before Scarpia)
On my knees I beg for mercy.
See me: *(sobbing)* like a beggar I lie before you.
(lifting her folded hands) Hear me, hear me. *(in despair)* I'm defeated.
I implore you. *(humbly)* Show me mercy.

SCARPIA

You're much too lovely, Tosca.
Such charming graces! Well then . . . it seems I can't best you.
You win your Mario; I, a single night's embraces!

TOSCA *(getting up, showing her contempt)*

No, no!
How I detest you.

SCARPIA

(a knock at the door)
Who's that?
(Spoletta enters, greatly agitated.)

SPOLETTA

Excellency, Angelotti killed himself
before we reached him.

SCARPIA

All right. We will hang his corpse on the gallows.
And how about his friend?

SPOLETTA

Il cavalier Cavaradossi? È tutto
pronto, Eccellenza.

TOSCA

(Dio, m'assisti!...)

SCARPIA

(a Spoletta)
Aspetta.
(a Tosca)
Ebbene?
(Tosca accenna di sì col capo e dalla vergogna piangendo si nasconde il viso)
(a Spoletta)
Odi...

TOSCA

(interrompendo, subito a Scarpia)
Ma libero all'istante
lo voglio...

SCARPIA

(a Tosca)
Occorre simular. Non posso
far grazia aperta. Bisogna che tutti
abbian per morto il cavalier.
(accenna a Spoletta) Quest'uomo
fido provvederà.

TOSCA

Chi mi assicura?

SCARPIA

L'ordin che gli darò voi qui presente.
(a Spoletta)
Spoletta: chiudi,
(Spoletta chiude la porta, poi ritorna presso Scarpia)
Ho mutato d'avviso.
Il prigionier sia fucilato...
(Tosca scatta atterrita)
attendi...
(fissa con intenzione Spoletta che accenna replicatamente col capo di indovinare il pensiero di Scarpia)
Come facemmo del conte Palmieri.

SPOLETTA

Un'uccisione...

SCARPIA

(subito con marcata intenzione)
... simulata!... Come
avvenne del Palmieri!... Hai ben compreso?

SPOLETTA

Ho ben compreso.

SCARPIA

Va.

SPOLETTA

You mean that man, Cavaradossi?
We shall proceed as you ordered.

TOSCA *(to herself)*

God in Heaven!

SCARPIA *(to Spoletta)*

One moment.
(to Tosca, in a low voice)
I'm waiting.
(Tosca nods "yes," then weeping for shame she buries her head in the cushions on the sofa.)
(to Spoletta) Listen.

TOSCA *(interrupting Scarpia)*

You promise he'll be free before morning?

SCARPIA *(to Tosca)*

That's more than I can do. I've never granted a pardon.
We must make it seem as though he was really put to death.
(indicating Spoletta) My man here will take good care of that.

TOSCA

How can I trust you?

SCARPIA

I will instruct him right now,
in your presence.
(turning to Spoletta) Spoletta, listen:
(Spoletta quickly closes the door and goes back to Scarpia. Scarpia gives Spoletta a significant glance; Spoletta indicates that he grasps Scarpia's idea.)
I am changing my orders.
Instead of hanging, we will shoot him.
However, we shall proceed as we did with Palmieri!

SPOLETTA

An execution?

SCARPIA *(suddenly, with clear intention)*

Without bullets! Just the same as with Palmieri!
You understand me?

SPOLETTA

I understand you.

SCARPIA

Go.
(Tosca, having listened eagerly, intervenes.)

TOSCA
Voglio avvertirlo
io stessa.

SCARPIA
E sia.
(a Spoletta) Le darai passo. Bada:
all'ora quarta.

SPOLETTA
Sì. Come Palmieri.
(Spoletta parte. Scarpia, ritta presso la porta, ascolta Spoletta allontanarsi, poi trasformato nel viso e nei gesti si avvicina con grande passione a Tosca)

SCARPIA
Io tenni la promessa...

TOSCA
(arrestandolo)
Non ancora.
Voglio un salvacondotto onde fuggire
dallo Stato con lui.

SCARPIA
(con galanteria)
Partir volete?

TOSCA
Sì, per sempre!

SCARPIA
Si adempia il voler vostro.
(va allo scrittoio: si mette a scrivere, interrompendosi per domandare a Tosca:)
Qual via scegliete?
(Mentre Scarpia scrive, Tosca si è avvicinata alla tavola e colla mano tremante prende il bicchiere di vino di Spagna versato da Scarpia; ma nel portare il bicchiere alle labbra, scorge, sulla tavola un coltello affilato ed a punta; dà una rapida occhiata a Scarpia che in quel momento è occupato a scrivere — e con infinite precauzioni cerca di impossessarsi del coltello, rispondendo alle domande di Scarpia ch'essa sorveglia attentamente)

TOSCA
La più breve!

SCARPIA
Dunque
Civitavecchia.
(scrivendo)
Sta bene?

TOSCA
Sta bene.
(Finalmente ha potuto prendere il coltello, che dissimula dietro di sè appoggiandosi alla tavola e sempre sorvegliando Scarpia. Questi ha finito di scrivere il salvacondotto, vi mette il sigillo, ripiega il foglio: quindi aprendo le braccia si avvicina a Tosca per avvincerla a sè)

SCARPIA
Ed ora, Tosca, finalmente mia!...
(ma l'accento voluttuoso si cambia in un grido terribile — Tosca lo ha colpito in pieno petto)

TOSCA

I want to tell him myself.

SCARPIA *(to Spoletta, pointing at Tosca)*

All right.
I've no objection.
(with great emphasis) That's all. At four, this morning.

SPOLETTA *(making his intention quite clear)*

Yes, just like Palmieri.
(Spoletta leaves.
Scarpia, near the door, makes sure that Spoletta has gone; then, transformed in gesture and expression, he approaches Tosca in a passionate outburst.)

SCARPIA

You see, I've kept my promise.

TOSCA

(stopping him)
Not completely. Give me something in writing
so that we can leave the country at once.

SCARPIA *(very courteously)*

You mean you want to leave us?

TOSCA *(with conviction)*

Yes, forever!

SCARPIA

Your wishes are my orders.
(goes to his desk and writes; looking up from his writing, he asks Tosca:)
Which way will you travel?

TOSCA

By the shortest.

SCARPIA

You mean by water?

TOSCA

Yes.
(While Scarpia writes, Tosca walks over to the table and lifts, with a trembling hand, the glass that Scarpia had filled. While doing so, she sees the knife on the table. After a furtive glance at Scarpia, who is still writing, she grasps the knife and, very cautiously, hides it behind her back, leaning against the table and still glancing at Scarpia.
Scarpia has finished writing the safe-conduct note. He puts his seal on it and folds it; opening his arms he goes towards Tosca to embrace her.)

SCARPIA

Maledetta!!

TOSCA

Questo è il bacio di Tosca!
(*Scarpia stende il braccio verso Tosca avvicinandosele barcollante in atto di aiuto. Tosca lo sfugge — ma ad un tratto ella si trova presa fra Scarpia e la tavola e vedendo che sta per essere toccata da Scarpia, lo respinge inorridita. Scarpia cade, urlando colla voce soffocata dal sangue:*)

SCARPIA

Aiuto . . . aiuto . . . muoio . . .

TOSCA

E ucciso da una donna . . . — M'hai assai
torturata?! — Odi tu ancora? . . .
Parla! . . . Guardami! . . .
Son Tosca, o Scarpia!

SCARPIA

(*fa un ultimo sforzo, poi cade riverso*)
Soccorso! . . .

TOSCA

(*chinandosi verso Scarpia*)
Ti soffoca
il sangue? . . . il sangue? . . . Muori! muori!! muori!!!
(*vedendolo immobile*)
Ah è morto! . . . Or gli perdono! . . .
E avanti a lui tremava tutta Roma!
(*Senza abbandonare cogli occhi il cadavere, Tosca va alla tavola, vi depone il coltello, prende una bottiglia d'acqua, inzuppa un tovagliolo e si lava le dita: poi va allo specchio e si ravvia i capelli. Quindi cerca il salvacondotto sullo scrittoio: non trovandolo, si volge e lo scorge nella mano raggrinzita del morto: ne toglie il foglio e lo nasconde in petto. Spegne il candelabro sulla tavola e va per uscire, ma si pente e vedendo accesa una delle candele sullo scrittoio, va a prenderla, accende l'altra, e colloca una candela a destra e l'altra a sinistra della testa di Scarpia. Alzandosi, cerca di nuovo intorno e scorgendo un crocifisso va a staccarlo dalla parete e portandolo religiosamente s'inginocchia per posarlo sul petto di Scarpia — poi si alza e con grande precauzione esce rinchiudendo dietro a sè la porta.*)

SCARPIA

Tosca! Now at last you're mine!
(Tosca stabs him)
(shouting) You assassin!

TOSCA *(shouting)*

That's the way Tosca kisses!

SCARPIA *(with a breaking voice)*

I'm dying ... help me!
(Staggering, he tries to get hold of Tosca, who withdraws in horror.)

TOSCA *(with hatred)*

Your own blood will choke you.

SCARPIA *(choking)*

I'm dying.
(tries in vain to rise, clutching the sofa)

TOSCA

It's Tosca who has killed you.
Now you pay for my torture!
(Scarpia makes one last effort, then falls on his back.)
Can you still hear me?
Answer! Look at me!
Look, Scarpia, it's Tosca!
Your own blood will choke you.
(bending over Scarpia)
Die in damnation, Scarpia! Die now!

SCARPIA

Ah.
(remains motionless)

TOSCA

He's dead! Now I forgive him.
(Without taking her eyes off Scarpia, Tosca takes the water pitcher, pours out some water, and cleans her fingers with a napkin; then she arranges her hair before the mirror.
Remembering the safe-conduct note, she searches the desk but does not find it; finally she sees it in the hand of Scarpia.
She lifts his arm which she lets fall again after having taken the safe-conduct note out of his hand; she hides the document in her bodice.)
This is the man before whom all Rome trembled.
(About to leave, she changes her mind. She takes the two candlesticks, lights them with the candelabra on the table and then extinguishes the latter.
She places the two candles on either side of Scarpia's head.
Looking around she sees a crucifix. She lifts it from the wall and, carrying it, she kneels religiously and puts the crucifix on Scarpia's chest.
Drums are heard in the distance.
She rises and leaves the room very cautiously, closing the door behind her.)

(Fast curtain)

ATTO TERZO

La piattaforma di Castel Sant'Angelo

A sinistra, una casamatta: vi è collocata una tavola, sulla quale stanno una lampada, un grosso registro e l'occorrente per scrivere: una panca, una sedia. Su di una parete della casamatta un crocifisso: davanti a questo è appesa una lampada. A destra, l'apertura di una piccola scala per la quale si ascende alla piattaforma. Nel fondo il Vaticano e S. Pietro.
È ancora notte: a poco a poco la luce incerta e grigia che precede l'alba: le campane delle chiese suonano il mattutino. La voce d'un pastore che guida un armento.)
(Un Carceriere con una lanterna sale dalla scala, va alla casamatta e vi accende la lampada sospesa davanti al crocifisso, poi quella sulla tavola: siede ed aspetta mezzo assonnato. Più tardi un picchetto, comandato da un Sergente di guardia, sale sulla piattaforma accompagnando Cavaradossi: il picchetto si arresta ed il Sergente conduce Cavaradossi nella casamatta, consegnando un foglio al Carceriere. — Il Carceriere esamina il foglio, apre il registro e vi scrive mentre interroga.)

CARCERIERE

Mario Cavaradossi?
(Cavaradossi china il capo, assentendo. Il Carceriere porge la penna al Sergente)
A voi.
(Il Sergente firma il registro, poi parte coi soldati, scendendo per la scala)
(a Cavaradossi) Vi resta
un'ora. Un sacerdote i vostri cenni
attende.

CAVARADOSSI

No. Ma di un'ultima grazia
vi richiedo.

CARCERIERE

Se posso . . .

CAVARADOSSI

Io lascio al mondo
una persona cara. Consentite
ch'io le scriva un sol motto.
(togliendosi dal dito un anello) Unico resto
di mia ricchezza è questo
anel . . . Se promettete
di consegnarle il mio
ultimo addio,
esso è vostro . . .

ACT THREE
Scene: Castel Sant'Angelo

(To the left a prison cell, a bench, a chair, a table, on it a lamp, the prison register and writing utensils. On the wall, a crucifix, with a light in front of it. To the right, the opening of a stairwell which gives access to the platform. In the distance, the Vatican and St. Peter's Basilica.
Night. A clear sky, sparkling with stars.
In the distance sheepbells are heard, gradually fading away.)

SHEPHERD

Wind, hear my sorrow, my sorrow and my sighing
(The bells, still farther away, are heard at irregular intervals.)
like leaves in autumn that fade and fall in dying.
(The bells are dying away in the distance.)
Say that our vows have not been broken.
Send me a token,
else I must die.
(The light is uncertain and grey; it is just before dawn.)
(Church bells at various distances.
A jailer, with a lantern, climbs up the stairs, enters the prison cell and lights the lamp before the crucifix, then the one on the table. He walks to the railing and looks down into the courtyard to see whether the firing squad and the condemned man are arriving. He meets a sentry who is crossing the platform; after having exchanged some words with him, he returns to the cell; sits down, waiting, half-asleep.
A group of soldiers, led by a sergeant, arrives on the platform, escorting Cavaradossi. The soldiers stand still while the sergeant leads Cavaradossi to the cell.
Seeing the sergeant, the jailer gets up and salutes; the sergeant hands him a sheet of paper which he examines. He sits down at the table, opens the register and writes, while speaking to Cavaradossi.)

JAILER

Mario Cavaradossi?
(Cavaradossi nods in affirmation.)
Sign here.
(He hands a pen to the sergeant, who signs the register and leaves, followed by his soldiers.)
(to Cavaradossi)
You have an hour.
A priest is waiting if you should like to see one.

CAVARADOSSI

No. But I'd like to ask you for one last favor.

JAILER

What is it?

CAVARADOSSI

I leave behind me someone I love and cherish.
I would like to say farewell in a letter.
(taking a ring off his finger)
All I have left of my earthly wealth
is this little ring.
If you will promise me to make certain
that my note is delivered, you may keep it.

CARCERIERE

(tituba un poco, poi accetta e facendo cenno a Cavaradossi di sedere alla tavola, va a sedere sulla panca)
Scrivete.

CAVARADOSSI

(si mette a scrivere ... ma dopo tracciate alcune linee è invaso dalle rimembranze)
E lucevan le stelle ed olezzava
la terra — e stridea l'uscio
dell'orto — e un passo sfiorava la rena.
Entrava ella, fragrante,
mi cadea fra le braccia
Oh! dolci baci, o languide carezze,
mentr'io fremente
le belle forme discioglea dai veli!
Svanì per sempre il sogno mio d'amore ...
L'ora è fuggita
e muoio disperato! ...
E non ho amato mai tanto la vita!
(scoppia in singhiozzi.)
(Dalla scala viene Spoletta accompagnato dal Sergente e seguito da Tosca: il Sergente porta una lanterna — Spoletta accenna a Tosca ove trovasi Cavaradossi, poi chiama a sè il Carceriere; con questi e col Sergente ridiscende, non senza avere prima dato ad una sentinella, che sta in fondo, l'ordine di sorvegliare il prigioniero.)
(Tosca vede Cavaradossi piangente, colla testa fra le mani: gli si avvicina e gli solleva colle due mani la testa. Cavaradossi balza in piedi sorpreso. Tosca gli presenta convulsa un foglio, non potendo parlare per l'emozione.)

CAVARADOSSI

(legge)
Franchigia a Floria Tosca ...

TOSCA

(leggendo insieme con lui con voce affannosa e convulsa)
e al cavaliere
che l'accompagna, —
(a Cavaradossi con un grido esultanza)
Sei libero!

CAVARADOSSI

(guarda il foglio; ne legge la firma)
Scarpia ...
Scarpia che cede? la prima
sua grazia è questa ...

TOSCA

E l'ultima!
(riprende il salvacondotto e lo ripone in una borsa)

CAVARADOSSI

Che dici? ...

TOSCA

Il tuo sangue o il mio amore

JAILER
(After a slight hesitation, he accepts and motions to Cavaradossi to sit down.)
All right, then.
(He sits down on the bench.
Cavaradossi is deep in thought; then begins to write.
He writes a few lines but, overcome by his memories, he interrupts his writing.)

CAVARADOSSI
I remember the star light
and the perfume of roses,
a garden gate that opened,
a footstep as soft as an angel's . . .
I felt her fragrant presence,
we were lost in each other.
A night of kisses, passionate caresses,
my hands were trembling
to hold your loveliness in sweet surrender.
Forever now my dream of love is ended,
and when the day breaks I die in desperation,
I die in desperation!
and never was so much in love with living,
in love with living!
(He bursts into tears, buying his face in his hands.
Spoletta comes up the stairs with the sergeant, followed by Tosca: the sergeant carries a lantern. Spoletta shows Tosca where she can find Cavaradossi, then calls the jailer; with him and the sergeant he walks down the stairs again, after having beckoned to the sentry to keep an eye on the prisoner.
Tosca, who has been in a state of great excitement, sees Cavaradossi crying. She rushes up to him, but unable to speak for emotion, she raises his head with her hands and shows him the safe-conduct note. Cavaradossi, seeing Tosca, gets up in great surprise, then reads the document.)
The bearer, Floria Tosca
and her companion may cross the border.

TOSCA *(with enthusiasm)*
You're safe at last!

CAVARADOSSI
(looks and reads the signature)
Scarpia, granting a pardon?
(with an intent look on Tosca)
I'm sure that must be the first time!

TOSCA
(taking back the safe-conduct note)
Also the last!

CAVARADOSSI
What happened?

TOSCA *(in an outburst)*
"Love me, Tosca, or Mario must die."

volea. Fur vani scongiuri e pianti.
Invan, pazza d'orror,
alla Madonna mi volsi ed ai Santi...
L'empio mostro
Dicea: già nei cieli
il patibol le braccia leva!
Rullavano i tamburi...
Rideva, l'empio mostro... rideva...
già la sua preda pronto a ghermir!
"Sei mia?" — Si. — Alla sua brama
mi promisi. Lì presso
luccicava una lama...
Ei scrisse il foglio liberator,
venne all'orendo amplesso...
Io quella lama gli piantai nel cor.

CAVARADOSSI

Tu?... di tua man l'uccidesti! — tu pia,
tu benigna — e per me!

TOSCA

N'ebbi le mani
tutte lorde di sangue!...

CAVARADOSSI

(prendendo amorosamente fra le sue le mani di Tosca)
Oh! salvatrice!
O dolci mani mansuete e pure
o mani elette a bell' opre e pietose,
a carezzar fanciulli, a coglier rose,
a pregar, giunte, per l'altrui sventure,
dunque in voi, fatte dall'amor secure,
giustizia le sue sacre armi depose?
Voi deste morte, o man vittoriose,
o dolci mani mansuete e pure!...

TOSCA

(svincolando le mani)
Senti... l'ora è vicina; io già raccolsi
(mostrando la borsa)
ore e gioielli... una vettura è pronta.
Ma prima... ridi amor... prima sarai
fucilato — per finta — ad armi scariche.
Simulato supplizio. Al colpo... cadi.
I soldati sen vanno — e noi siam salvi!
Poscia a Civitavecchia... una tartana...
e via pel mar!

CAVARADOSSI

Liberi!

In vain did I kneel before him.
In vain, maddened with fear,
I offered prayers up to God to implore Him.
How he laughed when he told me:
"When the day breaks, they'll prepare him to mount the gallows."
I heard a muffled drum roll
and, laughing, how the monster was laughing,
waiting to lay his hands on his prey.
"You're mine now!" Yes.
I let him think that I was yielding.
And then I saw a knife on the table.
He signed the paper that set us free.
As he approached to kiss me,
I plunged the knife into his evil heart.

CAVARADOSSI

You?
It was you who destroyed him?
My darling, so gentle and so kind?

TOSCA

Yes, I have killed him.
My hands both are bloodstained.

CAVARADOSSI

(taking Tosca's hands in his own)
Your hands, so lovely, lovelier than flowers,
were made for labors of devout dedication;
to soothe a crying child and bring it consolation,
to pray for sunshine through wind and showers.
In these hands steadied by a lover's powers,
the Lord has laid the weapon of liberation!
You took his life with a holy exultation.
Your hands so lovely, lovelier than flowers.

TOSCA

(withdrawing her hands)
Listen, there's not much time left. *(pointing to her bag)*
I brought some money, also my jewels.
A carriage will be waiting.
But first, I know you will laugh,
first they will shoot you for treason!
For Scarpia must keep up appearances.
Yes, a mock execution! They'll fire . . . fall down.
They will leave soon thereafter.
We'll be united and free forever.
Once we have crossed the border
we'll find a sailboat and off to sea!

CAVARADOSSI

Liberty!

TOSCA

Liberty!

CAVARADOSSI

You and I.

TOSCA

Chi si duole
in terra più? Senti effluvi di rose?...
Non ti par che le cose
aspettan tutte innamorate il sole?...

CAVARADOSSI

(colla più tenera commozione)
Amaro sol per te m'era il morire
Da te prende la vita ogni splendore,
all'esser mio la gioia ed il desire
nascon di te, come di fiamma ardore.
Io folgorare i cieli e scolorire
vedrò nell'occhio tuo rivelatore,
e la beltà delle cose più mire
avrà solo da te voce e colore.

TOSCA

Amor che seppe a te vita serbare
ci sarà guida in terra, in mar nocchiere
e vago farà il mondo a riguardare.
Finchè congiunti alle celesti sfere
dileguerem, siccome alte sul mare
a sol cadente, nuvole leggere!
(rimangono commossi, silenziosi: poi Tosca, chiamata dalla realtà delle cose, si guarda attorno inquieta)
E non giungono...
(si volge a Cavaradossi con premurosa tenerezza)
Bada!...
al colpo egli è mestiere
che tu subito cada
per morto.

CAVARADOSSI

(la rassicura)
Non temere
che cadrò sul momento — e al naturale.

TOSCA

(insistendo)
Ma stammi attento — di non farti male!
Con scenica scienza
io saprei la movenza...

CAVARADOSSI

(la interrompe, attirandola a sè)
Parlami ancor come dianzi parlavi,
è così dolce il suon della tua voce!

TOSCA

(si abbandona quasi estasiata, quindi a poco a poco accalorandosi)
Uniti ed esulanti
diffonderan pel mondo i nostri amori
armonie di colori...

TOSCA

TOSCA

All this horror left behind.
Gone the sorrow that bound us.
Don't you feel how all around us dreams of beauty,
trembling before the sunrise?

CAVARADOSSI *(with tenderest emotion)*

The thought of dying tore my heart asunder,
to part from you, who gives my life its splendor.
It's you that fills my life with joy and wonder.
Love is the light that makes the dark surrender.
Like glittering stars when winter's night is falling,
your radiant eyes are full of revelation.
All things that beauty has rendered enthralling,
in your eyes they find their consecration.

TOSCA

My love that saved your life with its devotion
will be a shining light wherever we go.
Love will make us see
the world with a new emotion,
till to the sinking sun we'll be ascending;
freed from all bonds,
like clouds that float above the ocean.
(as though in a vision)
There will be only happiness unending.
*(They remain in silence, moved.
Brought back to reality, Tosca looks around nervously.)*
They're not coming yet.
(to Cavaradossi, with great tenderness)
Mario, remember you must pretend
they are shooting you in earnest.

CAVARADOSSI *(sadly)*

I'll remember.
I will fall, when they fire, just as you told me.

TOSCA *(urgently)*

But please be careful, don't get hurt in falling!
All actors can do it.
If I only could show you.

CAVARADOSSI *(interrupts her, drawing her towards him)*

Tell me again that our love is forever.
It is so sweet to hear you make that promise.

TOSCA *(with almost ecstatic abandon)*

United and enchanted, guarding the flame
that now is only ember,
our love will remember . . .

CAVARADOSSI

(*esaltandosi*)
ed armonie di canti!

TOSCA — CAVARADOSSI

(*con grande entusiasmo*)
Trionfal di nova
speme l'anima
freme in celestial
crescente ardor.
ed in armonico vol
già l'anima va
all'estasi d'amor.

TOSCA

Gli occhi ti chiuderò con mille baci
e mille ti dirò nomi d'amore.
(*Frattanto dalla scaletta è salito un drappello di soldati: lo comanda un Ufficiale, il quale schiera i soldati nel fondo: seguono Spoletta, il Sergente, il Carceriere. — Spoletta dà le necessari istruzioni. Il cielo si fa più luminoso; è l'alba: suonano le 4. Il Carceriere si avvicina a Cavaradossi e togliendosi il berretto gli indica l'Ufficiale.*)

CARCERIERE

L'ora!

CAVARADOSSI

Son pronto.
(*Il Carceriere prende il registro dei condannati e parte dalla scaletta*)

TOSCA

(*a Cavaradossi, con voce bassissima e ridendo di soppiatto*)
(Tieni a mente: al primo
colpo, giù . . .)

CAVARADOSSI

(*sottovoce, ridendo esso pure*)
(Giù).

TOSCA

(Nè rialzarti innanzi
ch'io ti chiami).

CAVARADOSSI

(No, amore!)

TOSCA

(E cadi bene).

CAVARADOSSI

(Come la Tosca in teatro).

TOSCA

(non ridere . . .)

CAVARADOSSI

(*facendosi cupo*)
(Così?)

TOSCA

(Così).
(*Cavaradossi segue l'Ufficiale dopo aver salutato Tosca, la quale si colloca a sinistra nella casamatta, in modo però di poter spiare quanto succede sulla piatta-*

TOSCA AND CAVARADOSSI *(in exaltation)*

... that the hope we created never can die!
(A firing squad appears on the stairs, commanded by an officer; Spoletta, the sergeant and the jailer follow. Spoletta gives instructions.)
(with great enthusiasm) You and I.
Our faith is growing
stronger in knowing:
when we are dead our love lives on.
Love that is greater than death
will shine in the dark, long after we are gone.
(The sky is getting lighter: dawn.)

TOSCA

Soon I will close your eyes with tender kisses,
and whisper words of love into your ear.

JAILER

(Walking up to Cavaradossi he takes off his cap, points to the officer; with the register under his arm, he descends the stairs, after having asked)
Ready?
(The clock strikes four.)

CAVARADOSSI

I'm ready.

TOSCA

(to Cavaradossi, under her breath, and almost laughing)
Now remember you hear a volley: Fall!

CAVARADOSSI *(in a low voice, also laughing)*

Yes.

TOSCA

Do not make any move until I call you!

CAVARADOSSI

No, my darling.

TOSCA

Be careful falling.

CAVARADOSSI *(smiling)*

Like Floria Tosca, the actress?

TOSCA *(seeing him smile)*

No laughing, now!

CAVARADOSSI *(seriously)*

Like this?

TOSCA

Like this.
(Cavaradossi, having said farewell to Tosca, follows the officer; Tosca remains in the cell. She is in a position that allows her to see what is happening on the platform.

forma. Essa vede l'Ufficiale ed il Sergente che conducono Cavaradossi presso al muro di faccia a lei: il Sergente vuol porre la benda agli occhi di Cavaradossi: questi, sorridendo, rifiuta. — Tali lugubri preparativi stancano la pazienza di Tosca.)

TOSCA

Com'è lunga l'attesa!
Perchè indugiano ancor?... Già sorge il sole...
Perchè indugiano ancora?... è una commedia,
lo so... ma questa angoscia eterna pare!...
(l'Ufficiale e il plotone dei soldati, impartendo gli ordini relativi)
Ecco!... apprestano l'armi... com'è bello
il mio Mario!...
(vedendo l'Ufficiale che sta per abbassare la sciabola, si porta le mani agli orecchi per non udire la detonazione; poi fa cenno colla testa a Cavaradossi di cadere, dicendo)
Là! muori!
(vedendolo a terra gli invia colle mani un bacio)
Ecco un artista!...
(Il Sergente si avvicina al caduto e lo osserva attentamente: Spoletta pure si è avvicinato; allontana il Sergente impedendogli di dare il colpo di grazia, quindi copre Cavaradossi con un mantello. L'Ufficiale allinea i soldati, il Sergente ritira la sentinella che sta in fondo, poi tutti, preceduti da Spoletta, scendono la scala. Tosca è agitatissima: essa sorveglia questi movimenti temendo che Cavaradossi, per impazienza, si muova o parli prima del momento opportuno.)
(a voce repressa versa Cavaradossi)
O Mario, non ti muovere...
Ma già s'avviano... taci! vanno... scendono.
(vista deserta la piattaforma, va ad scoltare presso l'imbocco della scaletta: vi si arresta trepidante, affannosa, prendole ad un tratto che i soldati, anzichè allontanarsi, ritornino sulla piattaforma — di nuovo si volge a Cavaradossi, con voce bassa)
Ancora non ti muovere...
(ascolta — si sono tutti allontanati, va al parapetto e cautamente sporgendosi, osserva di sotto)
Or varcano il cortile...
(corre verso Cavaradossi)
Mario, su, presto! Andiamo!... andiamo!... Su!
(si china per aiutare Cavaradossi a rialzarsi: a un tratto dà un grido soffocato di terrore, di sorpresa e si guarda le mani colle quali ha sollevato il mantello)
Del sangue?!
(si inginocchia, toglie rapidamente il mantello e balza in piedi livida, atterita)
Morto!... morto!...
(con scomposte parole, con sospiri, singhiozzi si butta sul corpo di Cavaradossi, quasi non credendo all'orribile destino)
O Mario... morto? tu? così? Finire
così?... così?... povera Floria tua!!
(intanto dal cortile al disotto del parapetto e su dalla piccola scala arrivano prima confuse, poi sempre più vicine le voci di Sciarrone, di Spoletta e di alcuni soldati)

LA VOCE DI SCIARRONE

Vi dico, pugnalato!

She sees the officer and the sergeant who lead Cavaradossi to the opposite wall. The sergeant wants to blindfold Cavaradossi who, smilingly, refuses. Tosca's patience is sorely tried by these lugubrious preparations.)
How I wish it were over!
Why this terrible wait?
(It is almost daylight.)
It's almost morning.
What on earth do they wait for?
It's only acting, I know,
and yet this waiting makes me tremble.
(The officer and the sergeant order the soldiers to take up their positions.)
There now, it seems they are ready.
He is handsome, my Mario!
(Seeing the officer about to lower his sabre, Tosca raises her hands to her ears so as not to hear the shots; she beckons to Cavaradossi to fall down, saying:)
There! Fall now!
(The officer lowers his sabre; the shots ring out.)
(Seeing Cavaradossi on the ground, she throws him a kiss with her hand.)
He's such an artist.
(The sergeant approaches Cavaradossi and scrutinizes his body: Spoletta stops the sergeant from giving Cavaradossi the coup de grace. The officer orders the soldiers to fall in line again; the sergeant relieves the rear sentry; all, preceded by Spoletta, walk down the stairs.
Tosca, in great agitation, has closely watched all these moves, fearing that Cavaradossi, getting impatient, might move or get up too early.)
Be careful, do not move too soon.
They're leaving now . . . quiet.
They are leaving now.
(Suspecting that the soldiers might yet return, she again addresses Cavaradossi.)
One moment, do not move too soon.
(Tosca rushes to the parapet and, leaning over, looks down.
Going closer to Cavaradossi, almost spoken.)
Now they're gone. Mario, Mario.
Get up. Let's go!
(disturbed, she touches him.)
Come, come. Mario! Mario!
(uncovering the corpse)
(an outcry) Ah! *(in despair)* Mario!
(between sighing and sobbing) They killed him! Mario!
(throwing herself on Cavaradossi's body)
You: like this! Is this how it ends?
(embracing Cavaradossi's lifeless form)
Dead . . . Mario, Mario!
(prolonged cries from a distance)

SCIARRONE

I tell you: he was murdered!

VOCI CONFUSE

Scarpia?...

LA VOCE DI SCIARRONE

Scarpia.

LA VOCE DI SPOLETTA

La donna è Tosca!

VARI VOCI PIU VICINE

Che non sfugga!

LA VOCE DI SPOLETTA

(più vicina)
Attenti
là — allo sbocco delle scale...
(Spoletta apparisce dalla scala, mentre Sciarrone dietro a lui gli grida additando Tosca)
È lei!

SPOLETTA

(gettandosi su Tosca)
Ah! Tosca, pagherai
ben cara la sua vita...
(Tosca balza in piedi e invece di sfuggire Spoletta, lo respinge violentemente, rispodendogli:)

TOSCA

Colla mia!
(all'urto inaspettato Spoletta dà addietro e Tosca rapida gli sfugge, passa avanti Sciarrone ancora sulla scala e correndo al parapetto si getta nel vuoto gridando:)
O Scarpia, avanti a Dio!... Avanti a Dio!
(Sciarrone ed alcuni soldati, saliti confusamente, corrono al parapetto e guardano giù. Spoletta rimane esterrefatto, allibito.)

FINIS

SPOLETTA AND SCIARRONE *(yelling)*

Scarpia?

SCIARRONE

Scarpia.

TOSCA *(crying)*

Mario! What shall I do without you?

SPOLETTA

Murdered by Tosca!

SCIARRONE AND CHORUS

We must catch her.
At once, post a guard at every exit.
(Weeping desperately, Tosca throws herself on Cavaradossi's corpse.)
(A great noise is heard from downstairs.
Spoletta and Sciarrone appear at the top of the stairs.)

SCIARRONE *(pointing to Tosca, cries)*

She's here!

SPOLETTA

Ah, Tosca! We will make you pay for Scarpia's murder.
(As Spoletta tries to seize Tosca, she jumps to her feet, pushes him back violently so as to make him almost fall down the stairs; she runs to the parapet and, shouting:)

TOSCA

With my life! Oh, Scarpia,
the Lord will judge.
(She throws herself over the parapet. Sciarrone and a few soldiers, in confusion, rush to the parapet and look down. Spoletta stands there, horrified and trembling.)

(Fast curtain)